PRAISE FOR

WELL DONE

"I continue to be grateful for Reagan Rose's ministry to the church. His commitment to helping believers think through the practical steps of obedience to the Christian faith is commendable. His latest book, *Well Done: A Strategy for Life Stewardship*, does not disappoint. Reagan's argument is that all of the Christian life is stewardship, and he makes his argument biblically and convincingly. Not only does he explore Scripture's teaching on the concept of stewardship, he also offers practical encouragements for how we can be faithful to that charge. This book is well-written, helpful, and uplifting. I commend it to you warmly."

— Nate Pickowicz
Pastor of Harvest Bible Church in Gilmanton Iron Works, NH
Author of *How to Eat Your Bible*

T0054550

CHRISTIAN LIVING

Well Done

A Strategy for Life Stewardship

REAGAN ROSE

PUBLICATIONS

Fort Washington, PA 19034

Well Done: A Strategy for Life Stewardship
The Institute for the Christian Life Series

Published by CLC Publications

USA: P.O. Box 1449, Fort Washington, PA 19034
www.clcpublications.com

UK: Kingsway CLC Trust
Unit 5, Glendale Avenue, Sandycroft, Flintshire, CH5 2QP
www.equippingthechurch.com

ISBN (paperback): 978-1-61958-367-2
ISBN (ebook): 978-1-61958-376-4

Printed in the United States of America

Unless otherwise noted, Scripture quotations are from the New American Standard Bible® (NASB), Copyright © 1960, 1962, 1963, 1968, 1971, 1972, 1973, 1975, 1977, 1995 by The Lockman Foundation. Used by permission. www.Lockman.org

Italics in Scripture quotations, if not original to the NASB, are the emphasis of the author.

CONTENTS

SERIES FOREWORD

THE INSTITUTE FOR THE CHRISTIAN LIFE SERIES

From the time the Lord called me to Grace Community Church, I have had two primary goals: to preach the Word of God faithfully (2 Tim. 4:2) and to entrust the truth to faithful men (2:2). In keeping with those priorities, The Master's Seminary has played a key role in training future pastors to handle the Word accurately and defend its truth boldly. These Master's students have gone out to serve and shepherd churches across the nation and around the world.

Several years ago, to assist these faithful pastors in their shepherding work, the seminary created a lay-training program, comprised of online video courses. The Institute for the Christian Life (which was originally called the Institute for Church Leadership) is designed to train lay people in four fundamental categories: Bible Knowledge, Sound Doctrine, Christian Living, and Shepherding Care.

The ICL is designed to bring biblical training, theological instruction, and practical ministry into the pew and the living room—making these indispensable tools accessible to believers at all levels of spiritual maturity and church leadership. This book series complements those online courses, as an aid for small group discussion and individual study.

My prayer for you as you read this book, and engage with the corresponding video content through the ICL, is that you would grow in the grace and knowledge of the Lord Jesus Christ. As the apostle Paul expressed in Ephesians 1:18–19, "I *pray that* the eyes of your heart may be enlightened, so that you will know what is the hope of His calling, what are the riches of the glory of His inheritance in the saints, and what is the surpassing greatness of His power toward us who believe."

John MacArthur
Pastor, Grace Community Church, Sun Valley, California
Chancellor, The Master's University and Seminary

7

EDITORIAL PREFACE

IN THE LAST CENTURY, the word "stewardship" has become synonymous with "financial stewardship" in the church. And while we can give thanks that believers are learning principles of fiscal responsibility and generosity, have we been underselling the doctrine of stewardship by primarily applying it to money.

In *Well Done: A Strategy for Life Stewardship* Reagan Rose provides an exposition of the Bible's teaching on stewardship, giving particular attention to Jesus' parable of the talents in Matthew 25. This survey of stewardship will leave even the most seasoned believer with a greater appreciation for the scope of their calling from God to be a steward—a calling that goes far beyond money matters.

With deep insights and highly practical application, Rose holds a lens for the Christians life that lends purpose and dignity to everything from work to time management, relationships to abilities, and every aspect of life in between. *Well Done* will increase your respect and gratitude for the incredible responsibility and privilege it is to be a servant of God.

Peter Sammons, PhD
Faculty Associate in Systematic Theology
The Master's Seminary

INTRODUCTION

"I WANT TO SERVE GOD."

That was the answer the young man gave me. We were sitting across from one another at a coffee shop on his college campus. At the time, I was serving as a campus minister at Ben's university, and he had asked me to join him for coffee. He said he wanted to talk about how to be more serious about his Christian walk.

That statement of his was in answer to the question I had just asked him. "What do you want to do with your life?"

Trying to probe a bit deeper, I asked what I thought was a rather innocuous question, "What do you mean by 'serve God'"?

"I . . ." He paused. "I guess I don't really know," he confessed. "I don't think I'm called to be a pastor or anything. Everyone says we're supposed to serve God. But I guess I don't really know what that looks like. How do we serve God?"

Then it was my turn to struggle for an answer. What does it really mean to serve God? Or asked a different way, how are we supposed to think about the Christian life? These sound like simple questions, and they invite simple answers. But as with many things in the church, we've learned to readily supply the "right answer." But when pressed, we struggle to define what we really mean. What exactly does it look like for a normal Christian to serve God in every aspect of his or her life? That's the question this book tries to answer.

In the twenty-fifth chapter of the Gospel of Matthew, Jesus gave us an illustration of what it means to serve God. And it is rich with meaning. This metaphor perfectly encapsulates our responsibility before God as Christians awaiting Christ's return. But sadly, this teaching has too frequently been robbed of its power in the modern church due to overly narrow interpretations that pigeonhole its application to just one tiny sliver of our lives.

I'm talking about the parable of the talents. In this extended metaphor, Jesus used the relationship of a steward and master to illustrate what the relationship between Jesus Christ and His followers would look like between His first and second coming. In a word, it's all about stewardship. Too often, when we Christians talk about stewardship, we only think in terms of financial stewardship. But the stewardship paradigm is one of the most helpful frameworks through which we can view the Christian life.

So, this is a book about stewardship, but this is not a book about money. Though we will talk about financial stewardship, our aims are more holistic. Randy Alcorn summed up the scope of stewardship best when he wrote, "Stewardship is not a subcategory of the Christian life. Stewardship is the Christian life."[1] This is a book about total life stewardship.

There is no higher honor and no more important responsibility than to be a steward in the house of the King of kings. And the purpose of this book is to encourage you from the Scriptures to take life stewardship seriously as well as to give you some practical resources for how to execute that mission faithfully in every area of your life.

In part one, we do a verse-by-verse study of the parable of the talents in Matthew 25:14–30 to understand the breadth of Jesus's teaching on life stewardship. Over these first five chapters, we will look at the charge, the content, the compass, the character, and the compensation of stewardship. We will see just how radical and pervasive this call to responsibility really is. We'll see how stewardship touches every aspect of life, and how it imbues even the most mundane tasks with a higher purpose.

In part two, we will turn our attention to the practice of stewardship. There we will look at how stewardship affects how we use our time, talents, and treasure in the day-to-day routines of life. For each of these areas of life, we will examine the biblical principles that inform how we manage them, highlight three practical commitments that we must maintain, and suggest one habit which will enable us to uphold them more effectively.

I pray that this book will give you a new lens through which to view the Christian life, that it would fill you with excitement for the unique mission God has given you, and that it would help you more faithfully steward all that He has entrusted to you, for His glory and your eternal good.

---

1   Randy C. Alcorn, *Money, Possessions, and Eternity* (Wheaton, IL: Tyndale House Publishers, 2003), 463.

Part 1

The Call to Stewardship

1

THE CHARGE OF STEWARDSHIP

For it is just like a man about to go on a journey.

Matthew 25:14

D O NOT IRON WHILE WEARING."

I recently saw a shirt in the store with a warning label that read: "Iron before wearing." That's sound advice for getting the wrinkles out of a new shirt. But what made me laugh was that the manufacturers added this qualification: "Do not iron while wearing."

It makes you wonder if there's a story behind that warning label.

A group of lawyers in my home state of Michigan host an annual "Wacky Warning Label Contest" in which people submit the silliest warning labels they've come across. The submissions are then voted on by a panel of judges. Previous winners include labels such as, "Warning, harmful if swallowed" which appeared on a fishing lure; a utility knife with the label, "Warning: Blades are sharp"; and my all-time favorite, "Remove Child Before Folding," which was found on a stroller and inspired a book by the same title.[1]

It's easy to laugh at these comical warning labels. We think, "Are people really that dumb?" But the labels are there less for our protection and more for the manufacturer's protection. It our sue-happy society, a warning against ironing a shirt while wearing it really means, "If you burn your belly with a hot iron while wearing this shirt, it's not our fault."

"We are not responsible."

That phrase could be the tag line for our century. We live in an age that hates responsibility. Ours is a world of finger-pointing, buck-passing, and blame-shifting. We see it in the absurdly long "Terms of service" notices we ignore when installing a new app, the run around we get with a health insurance claim, or the warning labels on even the most harmless products.

---

1   "Wacky Warning Label Contest." Michigan Lawsuit Abuse Watch. https://www.lawsuitfairness.org/wacky-warning-label-contest (accessed Oct. 17, 2022).

But it's more than just corporations ducking lawsuits from litigious consumers. Our society's allergy to responsibility has also affected us as individuals. We're trained to always be on the lookout for potential scapegoats for our problems. If things aren't going our way, we have dozens of candidates to accuse. We can blame psychology, genetics, societal structures, the government, our families, or even the weather. It doesn't really matter who or what we blame, the important thing to remember is that it's never our fault.

We have become expert contestants in the blame game. Look at the fruit our responsibility-averse culture has born: skyrocketing abortion rates, rampant divorce, epidemic levels of fatherlessness, alcoholism, drug addiction, and worse. But our disdain for accountability drives us to more respectable diversions as well: endless entertainment binges, perpetual escape into fantasy worlds, video game addiction, or the most common (and most acceptable) addiction: hiding from our responsibilities by burying our faces in our phones and social media.

The Call to Take Responsibility

Indeed, we live in irresponsible times. But despite what the world around us does, we Christians are called to be people who take responsibility for our actions.

The Christian life begins with taking responsibility. When we come to the heavenly courtroom, we approach the bench with a plea of guilty. Repentance requires us to own our sin. "Yes, I did do that. Yes, I do deserve the consequences."

But the wonder of the gospel is that, if you have put your faith in Jesus Christ, the court rejects your guilty plea. For another person has already stepped forward to take the responsibility for your sin. Christ is your substitute. But that doesn't mean you can skip that first step of claiming culpability. Repentance requires an honesty about our sin, it requires taking responsibility. No man or woman ever began the Christian life by saying "It's not my fault." We begin by owning our sins, only to discover Christ has already owned them for us.

But this is where too many Christians stop short. We rightly acknowledge that our sins are forgiven in Christ, and His righteousness imputed to us by faith.

Although we wouldn't say it out loud, I fear many of us wrongly conclude that our part in the matter is now over. The debt is paid, so what else is there? Now we just sit around and wait for heaven, right?

The greatest joy we can obtain for ourselves and the highest honor we can give to God in the Christian life is still a matter of taking responsibility. And that is what life stewardship is all about.

STEWARDSHIP IS THE CHRISTIAN LIFE

This is a book about stewardship. More specifically, this is a book about life stewardship. Unfortunately, in most Christian circles the term stewardship has been reduced to indicate mere financial stewardship. And while money is an important a part of the stewardship equation, biblical stewardship encompasses a broader scope than just pecuniary matters.

So, what do we mean by stewardship? Here's one author's attempt to define it:

> From the biblical point of view stewardship is grateful and obedient response to God for His undeserved gifts, acknowledging Him as the ultimate owner and sovereign Lord of life, which is held as a trust issuing in the voluntary and responsible use of one's total self and possessions to the glory of God and in loving service to one's neighbor.[2]

Here's how another phrased it:

> Stewardship means man's exercise and administration of all his powers and possessions under God. The fact that a man is a steward means he is not the owner of the powers and possessions which he manages. To be a steward one must manage that which belongs to another. A steward is a representative of a higher administration.[3]

Those are helpful definitions. But to put it as simply as possible, being a steward means having responsibility over something that doesn't belong to you. That's it.

And as we'll see, our entire lives belong to God, which means everything in our lives is a stewardship. Christian stewardship, therefore, is simply a matter of what you do with the life God has entrusted to you. Stewardship is comprehensive. It's a term that can sum up the whole of our duty before God. Stewardship *is* the Christian life.

---

2 Paul Leonard Stagg, "An Interpretation of Christian Stewardship," in *What is the Church?* ed. Duke K. McCall (Nashville: Broadman Press, 1958), 148.

3 Kelsey, George D. "An Interpretation of the Doctrine of Stewardship," *Review & Expositor,* April, 1953, 186.

Watching for the King's Return

I have a three-year-old son, and like so many boys, he loves trucks. But he especially loves garbage trucks. That means trash day is his favorite day of the week. His room overlooks the street where the trash bins sit. So, every Tuesday morning, he eagerly stares out his window, watching and waiting for the garbage truck to arrive. He loves seeing those massive hydraulic arms lift our weeks' worth of refuse high in the air and dump it into the back of the truck. Nothing makes him happier.

But since he is a three-year-old boy, he also doesn't have the longest attention span in the world. Though he begins his watch with the best intentions, my son often grows bored and abandons his sentinel post at the window to play with toys or to look at a book. And on more than one occasion these distractions have caused him to miss seeing the garbage truck. By the time he hears the roar of the engine and runs to the window, it's too late. They've dumped the trash and are moving on. I hate seeing how disappointed he is when this happens. How awful to have a lack of watchfulness make you miss the thing you were most eager to see.

When Jesus was coming to the end of His teaching ministry, before His crucifixion and subsequent resurrection, He delivered what has come to be known as the Olivet Discourse. It's been given this name because He gave it "as He was sitting on the Mount of Olives" (Matt. 24:3). Jesus delivered this discourse in response to a question from His disciples, "Tell us, when will these things be, and what will be the sign of your coming and of the end of the age?" (24:3). Jesus' extended answer to this question is recorded in Matthew 24:1–25:46.

Jesus' Olivet Discourse was filled with final warnings, prophecies about what was to come, and encouragements to the disciples before His departure. In this discourse, Jesus told His disciples about the destruction of the temple (24:1–2), the signs of the end of the age (24:3–14), the coming tribulation with its false christs and false prophets (24:15–28), His return (24:29–31), and the need for vigilance (24:32–51). No wonder this section of Scripture has often also been termed "The Eschatological Discourse," for it focuses on things that are to come.

A lot is packed into chapters 24 and 25, but Jesus had one message He wanted the disciples to take away from all of it. And you can boil that takeaway down to just one word: watchfulness. Again and again, Jesus warned the disciples, "Be on the alert, for you do not know which day your Lord is coming," and "You also must be ready; for the Son of Man is coming at an hour when you do not think *He will*" (Matt. 24:42, 44). Jesus pictured His return, and the subsequent judgment, like the suddenness of the flood in Noah's day (24:37, 39), or like the surprise of a thief breaking in at night (24:43). If the homeowners had known the thief was coming, they would have prepared. The Olivet Discourse, then, is all about watchfulness.

The big takeaway for us is that we know Jesus is returning, but we don't know when. So, we must always be ready. But what does readiness look like? And how should we conduct our lives as we await His return? It's been 2,000 years since Christ uttered these words, and we are still waiting.

But are we still watching? Isn't it understandable if the watchman's vigilance wanes in the late hours of the night watch? This is the attitude Jesus was warning the disciples against. He wanted them to be ready. And the stakes for this watchfulness are much higher than merely missing seeing the garbage man.

The Parable of the Ten Virgins

To really drive this point home, Jesus told two parables that emphasized the importance of readiness for His return. In both stories there were consequences for those who were not ready and reward for those who were prepared. And like all parables, these are descriptions of what "the kingdom of heaven will be comparable to" (25:1).

First, in the parable of the ten virgins, Jesus told of a wedding and the ten virgins who were prepared to meet the bridegroom when he arrived. Half of them were characterized as wise for having planned ahead. They had enough oil for their lamps in case the bridegroom was delayed. The other half were called foolish for not having made such provision. Then, when the bridegroom suddenly arrived, the wise women went to celebrate the wedding feast while the foolish ones were still out looking to buy more oil (25:10). Their lack of watchfulness left them shut out of the wedding feast (25:11–12). And again, the point Jesus emphasizes to the disciples is, "Be on the alert then, for you do not the day nor the hour" (25:13). This is the point: We do not know when Jesus will return, so we must live every day ready for it. We must be watchful for the King's return.

The Parable of the Talents

The second parable Jesus told on the Mount of Olives was what has become known as the parable of the talents. This parable is the focus of the first part of this book. So, we will slow down and examine it much more closely over the next five chapters. But notice this key piece of context: since the parable of the talents is part of the Olivet Discourse, that means it is about the return of Christ and our need for watchfulness. This is not merely a story about being wise with your money, giving to charity, or kneeling to pray after a touchdown. Stewardship is about living faithfully in every aspect of life in eager expectation of Jesus' return.

Strap yourself into the disciples' sandals. They were sitting on the hill unaware of what would happen in the coming days. Very soon Jesus would be led away to be crucified, rise from the dead, and ascend into heaven. And then they would embark on a mission of proclamation that would turn the world upside-down.

No doubt in the days after those earth-shaking events the disciples reflected on all that Jesus had said in this discourse, now more fully understanding what He meant. Their Master who had been with them, led them, and taught them, was now gone. But He promised that He would return in the glory of the fullness of His kingdom to rule and reign on earth. It was now their responsibility to watch and wait—to take responsibility for what Christ had begun and now entrusted to them.

They were stewards called to be watchful. And as disciples of Jesus Christ, so are we. The parable of the talents shows us what watchfulness should look like in our own lives.

The Master's Journey

The parable began like the parable of the ten virgins—a description of what the kingdom of heaven would be like (Matt. 25:1). "For *it is* just like a man *about* to go on a journey" (25:14). The man, as we will see, was the master of a large estate. And in Luke's telling of a similar parable, He said the purpose of the man's journey was "to receive a kingdom for himself then return" (Luke 19:12).

The master in the story clearly represented Jesus who was going away but would return. That means these parables were not only relevant to the disciples in Jesus' day, but are also directly applicable to Christians living in this age.

Christ has ascended and we don't know how long He will be gone. We are living in the in-between. But we eagerly await His promised return. The question for us now is this: What will we, His servants, do while the Master is away? How will we conduct ourselves? How seriously will we take the responsibility He has entrusted to us?

If you are a follower of Jesus Christ, you are one of the servants in this parable. You've been entrusted with something that does not belong to you and charged to be watchful as you await Christ's return.

But if we are to faithfully execute on this charge of stewardship, we need to know exactly what we are supposed to be stewarding. In the next chapter, we will identify what Christ's servants have been entrusted with, how it differs from person to person, and how we can have confidence that we are investing our trust faithfully to make a good return for our Master.

Study Questions:

1. What's something you are responsible for that you wish you weren't?

2. What are some ways our society encourages us to be irresponsible?

3. How does thinking of your life as belonging to someone else change the way you treat it?

4. How often do you think about Jesus' return? Does it affect the way you live your day-to-day life?

5. Have you taken responsibility for your sin and turned to Christ in repentance and faith?

2

THE CONTENT OF STEWARDSHIP

Who called his own slaves and entrusted his possessions to them.

Matthew 25:14

SOME YEARS AGO, MY WIFE and I were asked to watch a couple's house while they were on vacation. We were thankful for house-watching opportunities because, at the time, we were living and traveling in our RV full time. As you can imagine, living that lifestyle can leave you feeling a bit cramped after a while. We welcomed any chance to stretch our legs in a home that was wider than eight feet and not on wheels.

The task was simple enough: watch our friends' pets—a dog and a cat—and look after the home for a week until they returned from their trip. They were also kind enough to let us bring along our own dog, Harvey (who relished the opportunity to have a yard to run around in). The two dogs got along wonderfully. And we quickly slipped into a new routine: Kim and I fed and let the animals out in the morning, locked up the house, and then went out for the day. We felt like we were on a little vacation of our own. That is until one infamous day at the beginning of July.

Would you like to know how I remembered it was the beginning of July? Because there were fireworks. Lots and lots of fireworks. And our dog, Harvey, did not care for fireworks.

Unbeknownst to us, while we were away from the house that day, some neighborhood kids were happily detonating unexploded ordinance from their Independence Day celebrations. Harvey, as it turned out, was not much of a patriot. Hearing the non-stop explosions sent him into a frenzy. And this must have gone on for hours while we were gone because when we returned to the house, it looked like a battlefield from the Revolutionary War.

Our dog had done everything he could possibly think of to try to escape the house and the sound of fireworks. He had scratched up windows, knocked over tables, chewed up furniture—he'd even ripped through the wires behind their TV. But the worst (and perhaps most impressive) feat of destruction was that he had nearly scratched a hole through their solid wood front door. I don't mean he put a few scratch marks on the door. This was like *The Shawshank Redemption*. He had burrowed the beginnings of a legitimate tunnel right through the door.

When we got back to the house, Kim and I stood in the doorway, mouths gaping. We were horrified. After we calmed the dog, we surveyed the damage. It was bad. Really bad. I still remember the horrible feeling of calling the homeowners to tell them what had happened. They had entrusted us with the responsibility of looking after their home, and we had failed them.

As we study stewardship, that's what we are talking about—taking responsibility for something that doesn't belong to us. It's a serious commitment. As we examine the parable of the talents to see what life stewardship looks like for a Christian, we ask, "What have I been called to steward?"

In the last chapter, we saw that the master in the parable—who represents Jesus—was going on a journey. The passage continues, "[the master] called his own slaves and entrusted his possessions to them. To one he gave five talents, to another two, and to another, one, each according to his own ability; and he went on his journey" (Matt. 25:14–15).

The question we will explore in this chapter is: What exactly has our Lord has entrusted to us? What do the talents in this parable represent? Because if we are to be faithful in our responsibility as stewards, we need to know the content of our stewardship.

What's a Talent?

Matthew 25:14 says the master "entrusted his possessions to them." The key word here is *entrusted*. The master charged the stewards with the care of something that belonged to Him. The verse calls this trust "talents" (25:18, 24, 25, 28). But what is a talent? And more importantly, what do these talents represent in the parable?

These talents are not talents like those we think of today. We use the term "talent" to refer to an individual's unique skill or ability. But in the ancient world, a talent was a unit of weight. The Hebrew word for talent is *kikkar*. But our English word "talent" comes from the Latin equivalent of the Greek *talanton* which means "a weight, something weighed."[1] Scholars'

---

1   "Weights and Measures," *Encyclopedia of The Bible*, https://www.biblegateway.com/resources/encyclopedia-of-the-bible/Weights-Measures (accessed Oct. 18, 2022).

opinions differ on how much a talent weighed. Perhaps the definition differed through time and from region to region. The talents referred to in our parable, however, were probably Greek talents. These talents weighed somewhere between sixty-six and three-fourths pounds and eighty-two and one-fourth pounds.[2] Most likely the talents in this story were talents of gold. So we're talking about around seventy-five pounds of gold. That's a lot of gold. Just a single talent of gold would have been a massive amount of money; equal to about twenty years wages for a laborer.[3]

Imagine that in today's money. That would be like if you made $50,000 per year and one day your boss said, "I'm going on an extended vacation for a couple of years. Can you take care of this for me while I'm gone?" Then he suddenly slapped a briefcase filled with *a million dollars* onto your desk and walked out of the building. That's just what it would have been like for the servant entrusted with just the one talent! This was no small responsibility the master was leaving to his servants. And that's why Jesus included this detail in the parable. It was to shock the disciples into realizing just how big of a responsibility He was leaving with them. This wasn't just watching the house for a week while He was away.

But here is where people tend to get this parable wrong and miss the bigger point Jesus was making. We read about how the servants in the story were entrusted with money, so we think, "Here is a parable about being responsible with our finances!"

But we forget this is a parable. The money represents something. We don't assume the parable of the ten virgins is about how to steward lamp oil do we? No, the oil represents something and so do the talents in this parable. The parable of the talents is not primarily designed to teach us a lesson about financial stewardship. Something bigger is going on here.

What do the talents represent then? By studying this parable and the other stewardship parables, I think we can draw at least three conclusions about what these talents were meant to illustrate.

First, remembering that the master represents Jesus, and the servants represent His disciples, we should note that the talents are something that rightly belong to Jesus and that He has entrusted to our care (Matt. 25:14–15). Second, the talents are something that we can invest and make a return

---

2   "Bible Weights and Measurements," Bible Hub, https://biblehub.com/weights-and-measures/ (accessed Oct. 28, 2022).

3   "Bible Weights and Measurements," Bible Hub, https://biblehub.com/weights-and-measures/ (accessed Oct. 28, 2022).

on for Him (Matt. 25:16–28). Third, the talents can be taken back by the master and given to another (25:28).

Finances certainly fit these three criteria, but more things can also be described using these measures. Also, the occasion and context of this parable gives us a clue as to the scope of its application. As we saw in the previous chapter, Jesus was preparing His disciples for His departure. So what was He leaving to their care?

I argue that the talents in the parable represent the portion of Jesus' slowly expanding kingdom that has uniquely been entrusted to each of Christ's followers. The Kingdom rightly belongs to Jesus, yet upon His departure He instructed his disciples to continue to proclaim the gospel, disciple believers, and faithfully obey Him so the Kingdom would continue to grow in the world (28:18–20; 13:31–32).

That is the charge. The King of kings has entrusted you to steward a valuable stake in His kingdom until He returns in glory. The talents make up the portion God has entrusted to each believer.

That should, frankly, strike us as an overwhelming responsibility. The notion that I'm to steward God's kingdom on earth should instill the same shock as if my boss entrusted me with a million dollars. How can I possibly fulfill this great duty?

But here again is where the parable of the talents is so helpful. The master in the story does not entrust any one disciple with his entire estate. Instead, he apportions differing amounts among them. The talents in the parable represent that unique calling God has given you. Each believer's stewardship will be unique to that person. And while we are not asked to carry the weight of the entire kingdom, this is still no small task. I am convinced that the talents apportioned to you entail the entire scope of your life. This is your mission.

Stewardship of these talents, then, is not just a matter of your money. It's about everything. This certainly includes your physical resources such as your home, cars, and property. But it also includes non-physical things such as your unique opportunities, your spiritual gifts, and your abilities. All these belong to the Master. All are on loan to you with the expectation that you will improve them and make a good return for His kingdom.

After all, everything we have really belongs to God, doesn't it? "For who regards you as superior? What do you have that you did not receive? And if you did receive it, why do you boast as if you had not received it?" (1 Cor. 4:7). Our bodies are the blood-bought property of Jesus, "Or do you not know that your body is a temple of the Holy Spirit who is in you, whom you have from God, and that you are not your own? For you have been bought with a price. So glorify God in your body" (1 Cor. 6:19–20). It makes sense that if all of our lives belong to God, then all of life is a stewardship.

AN UNEVEN DISTRIBUTION

The most striking thing about this parable is not that the master entrusted his stewards with so much, but that there is such a variance in what he entrusted to each one. "To one he gave five talents, to another two, to another one, to each according to his ability" (Matt. 25:15).

It doesn't seem fair. Why didn't the master take what he planned to entrust to the servants and split it three ways? Why does God gift us differently, entrusting some believers with great spiritual gifts or financial resources or natural talent, while He entrusts others with seemingly very little?

In the parable, the master owned the estate, so he could entrust the parts of it as he chose. It was his right. So it is with God. He can dole out talents however He likes. But a close examination of how the master in the parable distributed the talents can be instructive for us as we look at the unique way God has gifted each of us.

First, God gifts us differently in terms of amount. Every believer in the Lord Jesus Christ has at least some stewardship, even if it appears small. And let us not forget that even the smallest trust in the parable was still equivalent to a small fortune. Nevertheless, we tend to compare our gifts with others and grumble. It's easy to look at the abilities, wealth, or opportunities that God gives others and feel jealous. But God gives no little gifts. I'll say it again: *God gives no little gifts.* What you have been entrusted with is of inestimable value. And just because it is not the same as what another has been given does not excuse you from employing it wisely.

It's also important to remember that the smallness of your talent may actually be a blessing. We've all known people who have been given gifts that far exceed their ability to manage, and those stories never end well.

I once read about a man who made a business out of buying lottery winners out of their prize money. Often state lotteries offer the option of collecting a lump sum of money or to be paid out monthly over many years. The lump sum, however, is significantly less than the total that would be accumulated by collecting monthly payments over years. So this investor would reach out to winners of the state lottery and offer to take over their monthly payments in exchange for paying them a larger lump sum than the state would. That way, in the long run this investor made more money, and the lottery winner got a larger single payout. The investor kept up with the lottery winners he had bought out, and he was amazed to find that most of them ended up ruining their lives within two years of winning the lottery. Most of them became alcoholics or drug addicts, destroyed their closest relationships, and blew through their winnings in less than 24 months. They had been entrusted with more than they had the ability to handle.

When we are tempted to despise the smallness of the gifts God has given to us, we would do well to remember this: Our talents are a responsibility. A larger bank account is a larger responsibility. A great gift for speaking is a talent that must not be squandered. A unique set of experiences provides you with a unique skill set that must be used wisely. When you recognize that all that you have really belongs to God, you can humbly decide to make the most of whatever gift He gives you, trusting that the Master knows best how to delegate authority over His own estate.

Second, God not only entrusts us differently in terms of amount, but He also gives different types of gifts. The parable does not say this directly, it only speaks of different numbers of talents. But if the talents represent all that God entrusts to His people, we can safely observe that talents differ not only in amount but also in kind.

God's people differ in their giftings of intellect, physical prowess, opportunities, upbringing, and spiritual giftings. But these differences should never be the cause of jealousy or division within the church. Paul deals with this at length regarding differing spiritual gifts in First Corinthians 12–14.

Our Master does not gift us all the same way. But we all have the same implied requirement to "take care of this, use it well, be faithful." And one very humbling truth to remember when we are tempted to despise the smallness of our gifts is that God will judge us not according to the greatness of the talent, but according to how well we invest it. No matter what we've been entrusted with, our response should be the same: "I will be faithful." Because as we will see, when you are faithful over a little He will set you over much (Matt. 25:21).

THE DEPARTURE

Matthew 25:15 concludes abruptly; after entrusting talents to the stewards, the master departed: "Then he went on his journey." The absence of the master gives this parable its drama. There's always a temptation to slack off while the boss is gone. But the point of this parable is that everything hangs on our faithfulness in Jesus' absence. For only when he thinks no one is watching is the true character of a steward revealed.

Study Questions:

1. What do the talents in the parable represent?

2. What are some talents you believe God has uniquely entrusted to you?

3. Are you tempted to despise any giftings because they are not as great as what other believers have?

4. Can you think of a time when you felt jealous about the giftings or possessions of another Christian?

5. What are some areas of stewardship in which you believe you are being faithful right now? What's a talent you need to more faithfully steward?

3

The Compass of Stewardship

The LORD God took the man and put him in
the garden of Eden to cultivate it and keep it.

Genesis 2:15

We will return to the parable of the talents in the next chapter. But first we need to zoom out to see the full compass of the stewardship concept in the Bible. A thorough understanding of the total scope of stewardship requires that we go back to the very beginning, because stewardship didn't begin in the New Testament; stewardship started in the garden.

The concept of stewardship was not something Jesus merely borrowed from the first-century pagan culture to make a point. As R.C. Sproul noted, "The role of the steward was not something that just happened to emerge in the Greek system of management, nor was it something invented by the Egyptians in the time of Joseph. The steward's role derives from the principle of stewardship, which is rooted in the creation of mankind."[1]

The master and steward relationship has been part of mankind's calling since the very beginning. God created humans to be stewards of His creation. Stewardship, therefore, is baked into the very fabric of our being. It encompasses the whole of God's design for man from creation, through church age, and into our eventual role as stewards of a restored creation. As one author put it, "The Christian doctrine of stewardship has its roots in the doctrine of creation."[2] So we will begin our biblical survey of stewardship with creation.

---

1   R.C. Sproul "What Is Biblical Stewardship?" Ligonier Ministries, https://www. ligonier.org/learn/articles/what-biblical-stewardship (accessed Oct. 19, 2022)

2   Kelsey, George D., "An Interpretation of the Doctrine of Stewardship." *Review & Expositor,* April, 1953, 186.

STEWARDSHIP IN THE IMAGE OF GOD

Genesis 1:26–28 records the original purpose statement for mankind:

> Then God said, "Let Us make man in Our image, after Our likeness. And let them rule over the fish of the sea and over the birds of the sky and over the cattle and over all the earth, and over every creeping thing that creeps on the earth." God created man in His own image, in the image of God He created him; male and female He created them. God blessed them; and God said to them, "Be fruitful and multiply and fill the earth, and subdue it; and rule over the fish of the sea and over the birds of the sky and over every living thing that moves on the earth."

There's a lot packed into these three verses. Humans are:

1. Created in the image of God
2. Given dominion over the created beings
3. That dominion entails being fruitful and multiplying
4. It also entails subduing the earth and exercising dominion over every living thing on the earth.

In stewardship terms this passage means that God is the Creator—and thus Master of all creation—and He created human beings to be the stewards of His creation.

This call to fruitfulness, multiplication, filling the earth, and subduing it has variously been called the dominion mandate, the creation mandate, or the cultural mandate. Whatever you want to call it, this was the mission God set before mankind. We were called to be caretakers of His creation. We were stewards from the start.

STEWARDSHIP THROUGH THE AGES

The nature of our role as stewards, however, has changed through time. As God's covenant plans have unfolded, our responsibilities as stewards have looked slightly different in each of these epochs. Let's briefly survey how stewardship looked before the fall, after the fall, after the cross of Christ, and what the Bible reveals about what stewardship will look like in the restored creation.

Stewardship Before the Fall

From the very beginning God gave us, His image bearers, work to do in His creation. He made us stewards over the earth. From the charge to be fruitful and multiply (Gen. 1:28) to the command to work and keep the garden

(2:15), to the naming of the animals (2:19–20), inherent to the scope of humankind's calling is an overarching theme of creation stewardship. We were made to serve God by ruling over this planet under His charge.

The earth was given to us at the beginning not as our possession but as a trust. We ruled over it as God's vice-regents. After all, the earth is not ours, "The earth is the LORD's and all it contains" (Ps. 24:1). And as Sproul wrote, "It's not that God granted independent ownership of the planet to human-kind. It remains His possession. But God called Adam and Eve to exercise authority over the animals, plants, seas, rivers, sky, and the environment."[3]

So on the Mount of Olives, when Jesus was preparing His disciples to be faithful stewards of the Kingdom in His absence, He was not, in principal, giving a new command. Rather, He was calling them again to the purpose of every man and woman since the first morning light broke over the trees in Eden: "Take care of what I entrust to you." But what precisely was the nature of this stewardship?

Genesis 2:15 says Adam was put in the garden of Eden "to cultivate it and keep it." Other translations say, instead of cultivate, to "dress it," "tend it," or "till it." But the Hebrew verb literally translates to "serve it." Which is to say, humans were not to exploit it, abuse it, or trash it as though it belonged to us. At the time of creation, God's mandate for humanity was for us to reflect His image by caring for His creation in the same way He cares for us.

But this arrangement did not last long. For like the wicked steward in our parable, humans abrogated their responsibility and chose instead to rebel against their Master. Sin deeply affected our stewardship and our relationship to God, the creation, our fellow man, and even our work itself. But Adam's failure in stewardship did not remove humankind's duty to be faithful stewards. The command remained in place.

Stewardship After the Fall

Mankind's fall into sin is recorded in Genesis 3. As God's vice-regents the first man and woman had rules to abide by. It wasn't their garden, after all. And one of those rules was that they could eat from any tree of the garden, "but from the tree of the knowledge of good and evil you shall not eat" (Gen. 2:17). And you know the story—the serpent tempted the woman to eat from the tree and she shared it with the man (3:6).

This first sin plunged both mankind and the creation itself into pain and futility. Adam and Eve were exiled from the garden (Gen. 3:22–24).

---

3   R.C. Sproul, "What Is Biblical Stewardship?"

But not before God put a curse on both men and women (3:16–19). One thing that's easy to miss is that the curse for both men and women directly concerned their spheres of stewardship. Remember, the original call was to be fruitful and multiply. This call included many things, but it also included childbearing. And this is what God curses, "To the woman He said, I will greatly multiply your pain in childbirth, In pain you will bring forth children" (3:16). And for the man, the earth itself, which He was charged with stewarding, with all its plants and animals was cursed.

> Because you have listened to the voice of your wife, and have eaten of the tree about which I commanded you, saying, 'You shall not eat from it';
>
> > Cursed is the ground because of you;
> > In toil you will eat of it
> > All the days of your life.
> > "Both thorns and thistles it shall grow for you;
> > And you will eat the plants of the field;
> > By the sweat of your face
> > You will eat bread.   (3:17–19)

Humankind was placed under a curse, and the creation suffered with us. How interesting that God's curse for sin was a curse on our stewardship. It was a curse on the very things we were called to do in Genesis 1:26–28. It was a curse on our purpose as human beings. Yet, even while cursed, this original mandate was not set aside. Even in this cursed world, we are still beholden to that original call to be fruitful, multiply, and care for this earth. We know this because God repeated the same command to Noah and his sons after the flood. "And God blessed Noah and his sons and said to them, 'Be fruitful and multiply, and fill the earth'" (9:1).

Though the creation itself was corrupted by our sin and eagerly awaits the day when it will be free from this futility (Rom. 8:20–21), it is still ours to steward. As we'll see, our role as stewards of this earth has a bright future. It is tied to the spiritual stewardship we have been called to in this present age. But before our relationship to the earth could be restored, our relationship to God needed to be mended.

Stewardship and the Cross

The good news of the gospel is that Jesus came to live the perfect life Adam failed to live, and to die and subsequently defeat death in the place of all condemned sinners who put their faith in Him. Because of Jesus Christ believers are forgiven, declared righteous, and have the promise of an eternal inheritance.

However, many Christians miss that the cross also has implications for our purpose as stewards.

As we just saw, the command to steward this world was never removed, even after the fall. Rather after Jesus came, our stewardship actually expanded in scope. In the parable of the talents Jesus spoke about life stewardship regarding His kingdom, which was "not of this world" (John 18:36). The call to steward this kingdom means joining Jesus in this broadened mission.

Often when the apostle Paul spoke of stewardship, he used the term specifically to refer to the spiritual mission that God had entrusted to Him (1 Cor. 9:17; Col. 1:25). In his letter to the Ephesians, he talked about "administration of the mystery which for ages has been hidden in God who created all things" (Eph. 3:9). The English Standard Version uses the word "plan" here instead of "administration." The word translated "plan" is *oikonomia*, the same word normally translated as "stewardship." And just before Paul said this, Paul spoke of himself participating in "the stewardship of God's grace which was given to me for you" (Eph. 3:2).

This point is this: Christian stewardship in the new covenant era chiefly concerns our partnering with God to steward His plan for the redemption of the human race. In other words, it's about being faithful stewards of the gospel. This happens through proclamation of the gospel, as well as adorning it with our good works in living as people who truly have been transformed (Matt. 28:18–20; Titus 2:10). When Christians choose to live like Christians, we are acting like stewards.

Does the expansion of our stewardship include spiritual matters and Christ's plan for redemption set aside our original mission of stewarding the earth? Not at all. By the restoration of humans, the creation itself will also be restored. And a day is coming when we will again be stewards of a restored and renewed earth. A day is coming when work will no longer be frustrating, when our enmity with nature will be healed, when our service to the Lord again will be a joyous labor. But this future comes as we take up the mantle now in the church age to be stewards of the gospel. Paul showed that both humanity and creation long for redemption (Rom. 8:19–23).

> For the anxious longing of the creation waits eagerly for the revealing of
> the sons of God. For the creation was subjected to futility, not willingly,
> but because of Him who subjected it, in hope that the creation itself also
> will be set free from its slavery to corruption into the freedom of the glory
> of the children of God. For we know that the whole creation groans and
> suffers the pains of childbirth together until now. And not only this, but

we also ourselves, having the first fruits of the Spirit, even we ourselves groan within ourselves, waiting eagerly for *our* adoption as sons, the redemption of our body.

One more point of clarification before we move on. Some want to say, typically based on Colossians 1:20, that the purpose of Christ's atonement was not just for humanity's sins but also for the creation; that there were multiple intensions. But strictly speaking, this is not the proper way to speak of it.

The redemption and reconciliation of creation are by-products of God's reconciliation and redemption of humans, just as creation's curse was a by-product of mankind's disobedience to God. Man's sin created a rift between humans and God, and consequently God created a rift between people and creation in the Genesis 3 curse. The healing of this rift between humans and God, therefore, must be the prerequisite to healing the rift between people and creation.

Though every age calls for stewardship, the church age calls for a specific kind of stewardship. When Jesus uttered the parable of the talents, He had in mind the stewardship over His kingdom. The part of the story the disciples were in, and the part we are now in, is one of Kingdom expansion. Our particular stewardship in this era is one of nurturing and expanding the Kingdom rule of Christ in the hearts of all people. Once that tiny mustard seed grows to maturity, Christ will return, bringing the Kingdom to full fruition, stamping out the last enemy, death, making a new heavens and new earth, and taking His rightful seat on the throne in the New Jerusalem.

We must appreciate our role in the full scope of God's plan for redemption. This stewardship we've been entrusted with is a part of the kingdom of God. It's not some busy work God has given us to do, He's let us in on the mission—the greatest mission of all time.

Being a steward is the privilege of a lifetime. This should color how we think about every aspect of our lives. How am I using my time to improve the Kingdom? How am I reaching my neighbor with the gospel so that the Kingdom might gain another subject? How can I make the most of this opportunity to be fruitful in good works? How can I be a faithful steward?

And even at the risk of being labeled environmentalist hippies, we must not forget that though our primary calling in this age is a spiritual stewardship, our responsibility as stewards of creation is still in effect. Broken as it is by the curse, this is still God's planet, and we are still its caretakers. That doesn't mean we must all become vegetarians or tout the environmentalist agenda. Just because some pagans have elevated care of creation to the level of idolatry does not mean we should overreact and ignore the mandate God gave us from the beginning.

The Christian's care of creation looks different from the pagan's, however. Take our relationship with animals, for example. We understand that as stewards, it is perfectly lawful for us to use and enjoy animals, even to kill and eat them (Gen. 9:2–3). But at the same time Christians do not participate in cruelty toward animals because "A righteous man has regard for the life of his animal" (Prov. 12:10). The Christian's worldview towards creation is that of a steward. We recognize that the earth is our trust, but God gave it to us for our sustenance and enjoyment. God gave us this earth to care for and to use, but never to abuse.[4]

Stewarding the earth and stewarding the Kingdom are not competing missions. If you are a Christian who cares about this planet, your main objective should be getting the message of reconciliation to God to all nations. Because it is by the restoration of mankind's relationship with God that the creation itself will be set free from its futility. Nevertheless, even as we proclaim the gospel and live out its implications, every Christian must remember that the scope of our stewardship still concerns caring for the creation. Indeed, stewardship is about all of life, our health, neighborhood, the Kingdom, the earth, our finances, and much more. We are far too quick to compartmentalize our lives into secular and sacred when God has created us to be holistic stewards. And we must also remember that the story of stewardship is not over.

Stewardship and the New Earth

Many believers are surprised to learn that we will still work in heaven. Ask a hundred Christians to describe what heaven will be like, and you will likely hear more descriptions of floating on clouds than furrowing fields. But the

---

4   "Creation stewardship," is a term often used in more liberal theological circles to give biblical cover for the secular environmentalist movement. On the extreme end, members of the environmentalist movement seem to speak in pantheistic terms, worshipping the creation itself. Nevertheless, too often, Christians have overreacted against the claims and solutions proposed by environmentalists and have fallen into ignoring the very real biblical call to steward this planet. We can and should acknowledge that mankind has a responsibility before God to care for this earth, but we can do that without buying wholesale the agenda and claims of secularists. For a balanced and biblical survey of the topic, I recommend *A Different Shade of Green: Biodiversity and the Dominion Mandate* by Gordon Wilson (Moscow, Idaho: Canon Press), 2019.

Bible indicates that we will have work to do in the eternal state. In fact, we'll see in the coming chapters that part of the reward for faithful stewardship is more work in heaven.

The final destination for God's saints is not an ethereal spirit world, but a solid physical one—this earth, in fact, a restored creation. That's why passages such as First Corinthians 15 make such a big deal about the resurrection of our physical bodies. We will again walk in this earth, but it will be in renewed bodies on a renewed earth (Rev. 21:1).[5] But work will not be eliminated in that renewal. Work will be restored, not removed.

The biblical authors certainly do picture heaven as a place of rest (Rev. 14:13). But it will also be a place of activity and work. This may come as a disappointment when you first hear it. "What? I thought we were done with work!"

But take heart. The consequences of the curse will be lifted. That means work will be rewarding and enjoyable without the toil and hardship that came in Genesis 3. The thistles and thorns will be gone forever. When the Lord makes all things new, He will abolish every case of the Mondays.

Imagine all of things you enjoy about work: the satisfaction, the sense of progress, the knowledge that you have turned something that was disordered into a state of order. But imagine that without the confusion, sweat, or annoyance that seems part and parcel of all our work now. It will be more like that Edenic work that Adam and Eve enjoyed.

Work in the eternal state is something to look forward to, not to dread! Our labor will once more be "very good" when the taint of sin will no longer have any corrupting influence. Isaiah 65:21–23 describes life in the New Jerusalem, including the building of houses (65:21), farming (65:21), and work that is no longer in vain (65:23). Many things will end in heaven. Sinning will cease, war will cease (Mic. 4:3), and tears will cease (Rev. 21:4), but work will not cease. And neither will our stewardship.

Our original role as stewards will be brought to its full fruition on the new earth. The master and steward will work in one accord. "There will no longer be any curse; and the throne of God and of the Lamb will be in it, and His bond-servants will serve Him" (Rev. 22:3).

The Creator will once again walk with us in the garden of earth, and we

---

5   For a full treatment on heaven, the earth, and the eternal state, read *Heaven: A Comprehensive Guide to Everything the Bible Says About Our Eternal Home* by Randy Alcorn (Carol Stream, IL: Tyndale House Publishing, 2004). Chapters 41–44 address what the Scriptures teach about our activities in heaven.

will experience the joy of caring for His kingdom on earth without pain, toil, or rebellious hearts.

Conclusion

Stewardship is not something new. From the start, God made people to be stewards. Though we failed to fulfill that responsibility in the Garden and the very stuff of our stewardship was cursed, God's plan for the ages came to us in Jesus Christ, who healed the rift between man and God on that cross.

Now, in the church age, we continue our role as stewards by stewarding the mysteries of God. As we proclaim the gospel and live out its implications, we are outposts on earth for Jesus' kingdom. And one day that heavenly kingdom will be established with an earthly throne; the King of kings will seat Himself on the throne of David in the city of God. And that is when the real joy of stewardship will begin, for we will get to serve Him forever on a renewed earth.

What an exciting thing to look forward to! And what a great motivation to seek to be faithful stewards in this present age, as well. Because as we will see in Chapter 5, the scope of our individual stewardships in heaven will be directly tied to our faithfulness in stewarding what's given to us in this present life.

But before we go there, we need to zoom back in on the concept of stewardship as Jesus' disciples would have understood it in their context in the first century. They weren't thinking of creation stewardship when Jesus told the parable of the talents. More likely the disciples were picturing a household manager. The better we understand the role of a steward in the ancient world, the more fully we will see the picture of stewardship Jesus was painting in the parable of the talents, and we will better understand our own role as life stewards.

Study Questions:

1. What was mankind's first stewardship?

2. Do you think of your relationship to the earth as a stewardship? How might that change the way we think about nature?

3. How is the gospel a stewardship?

4. How can we balance our stewardship of spiritual matters with stewardship of more earthly matters, such as our health and jobs?

5. Does the idea of working in heaven excite you or frustrate you? Why?

4

THE CHARACTER OF STEWARDSHIP

*Immediately the one who had received the five talents went
and traded with them, and gained five more talents.*

Matthew 25:16

A PASTOR FRIEND OF MINE once told me about a man in his church who was respected by the whole congregation, but he turned out to not be who they thought he was. This man was quiet, but he attended every church gathering and was an accountant by trade.

The church desperately needed help managing their finances, so when the man volunteered to help with the accounting, they readily accepted. After a year of his keeping the books for the church they formally recognized his volunteer work and voted him in as a deacon.

Eventually this man began counting the offering each week. From all outward appearances, he did this job faithfully for almost forty years. The pastors, elders, and congregants were so thankful for his service that they publicly honored him many times throughout his tenure. When they built an addition onto their building, they dedicated it to him. Little did they know that over the course of his thirty-some years, this man had stolen almost two-million dollars from the church.

The theft was discovered when the church moved their books from paper processes to a digital accounting software. The contractor from the software company who was helping them migrate the old records to the new system started finding discrepancies. They found that this deacon they had presumed to be godly had been skimming money from the offering every week for nearly four decades.

When confronted by the pastor, this man—who was now in his seventies—showed no remorse. He spewed the vilest string of hateful profanities the pastor had ever heard. Then he proceeded to recount every sleight he felt "you Christians" had ever done to him over the years. Despite outward appearances, this deacon was bitter and hateful. He confessed that he was not a Christian. The elders and deacons held a meeting to explore where they had gone wrong. The church realized no one had really vetted this man. He was just a quiet guy who was good with numbers. They took his regular church attendance as evidence of faithfulness. Their mistake was that they had trusted him with a great responsibility before they knew his character.

When it comes to stewardship, perhaps nothing is more important than character. In the previous chapter, we looked at the scope of stewardship throughout human history. But in this chapter, we'll look more narrowly at what it meant to be a steward in the ancient world. What would Jesus' disciples have pictured when they heard Him telling this parable on the Mount of Olives? What were the qualities that a good steward would have had in that society? Stewards, after all, were often entrusted with massive responsibilities. So they had to be people of character. Understanding the context of ancient stewardship will give us greater insight into how we can be more faithful stewards in Christ's kingdom.

The Most Trusted Slave

One of the details people often miss in the parable of the talents is that the stewards didn't just work for the master—they were his slaves. This detail is not incidental to how Jesus would have us view our stewardship before Him.

The master-slave relationship is critical to understanding stewardship. Often, when we talk about stewardship in the church, we forget this. This is most obvious when we speak of stewardship in terms of opportunity, not obligation. But opportunity implies optionality. And we would be remiss to conclude that our role as stewards is anything but 100 percent mandatory.

The apostle Paul wrote, "It is *required* of stewards that one be found trustworthy" (1 Cor. 4:2). And when he spoke of his own stewardship of the gospel, Paul viewed it as a trust that he needed to fulfill whether he wanted to or not. "For if I do this voluntarily, I have a reward; but if against my will, I have a stewardship entrusted to me" (9:17).

He had a calling on his life and fulfilling that calling willingly was to his benefit. But even if he didn't do it willingly, he was still under obligation to God. Stewardship is a requirement not a choice. As Randy Alcorn put it, "Stewardship is the life calling of the servant. Resignation isn't an option."[1]

---

1   Randy Alcorn, *Money, Possessions and Eternity,* (Carol Stream, IL: Tyndale House, Publishers, 2021), 148.

Interestingly, though the parable of the talents is what most Christians think of when the topic of stewardship is mentioned, the word *steward* never appears in Matthew 25. Instead, the three men entrusted with the talents are six times referred to by the Greek word *doulos* which means "slave."[2] Why is this important? Because these were not mere employees of the master, and neither are we. They were slaves.

Throughout the New Testament the master-slave relationship is used to illustrate the relationship between Christ and His disciples. Unfortunately, modern English translations often blunt the force of this important biblical truth by translating the word *doulos* as "servant" rather than "slave."[3]

We certainly are servants of God, but that translation doesn't completely capture the force of the word *doulos*. If we merely think of ourselves as servants, we may think our service to the master is optional, even though it isn't. Many believers view stewardship is an voluntary extra, something only "super Christians" need to concern themselves with. But that is not the case.

When you confess Jesus as Lord, it isn't merely a formality or simply another name for the Christ. Calling Him "Lord" is acknowledging His right over your life. It is a humble recognition of your place in the master-slave relationship. A slave does not have rights. He or she belongs to the master. As the apostle Paul wrote, "You are not your own . . . For you have been bought with a price: therefore glorify God in your body" (1 Cor. 6:19–20).

What is the relationship between a slave and a steward? Though the parable of the talents did not use the term "steward," the responsibilities of the slaves in the parable perfectly fit the description of a steward in the ancient world. In Jesus' day, a steward was a slave who was entrusted with care of his master's household economics. In fact, the English word "economy" comes from the Greek word, *oikonomia*, meaning stewardship, administration, or economy.[4] A related word, *oikonomos*, referred to

---

2   K. H. Rengstorf, "δουλος" *Theological Dictionary of the New Testament* 2:261–81; Danker, Frederick W., Walter Bauer, William F. Arndt, and F. Wilbur Gingrich. *Greek-English Lexicon of the New Testament and Other Early Christian Literature.* 3rd ed. (Chicago: University of Chicago Press, 2000), 260.

3   For a fuller treatment on this subject see the book *Slave: The Hidden Truth About Your Identity in Christ,* John MacArthur, (Nashville: Thomas Nelson, 2012).

4   H. Seesman, "οικονομια" *Theological Dictionary of the New Testament* 5:119–56; Danker, Frederick W., Walter Bauer, William F. Arndt, and F. Wilbur Gingrich. *Greek-English Lexicon of the New Testament and Other Early Christian Literature.* 3rd ed. (Chicago: University of Chicago Press, 2000), 696.

the stewards themselves. That word consists of two parts: *Oikos,* meaning "house" or "household" and *nomos,* meaning "law." So *oikonomos* literally means "house law" or "household management." The *oikonomia,* then, was that which the *oikonomos* had been charged to look after; the stewardship and the steward.

This convention was common in ancient times before the Hellenistic world. Consider Joseph, for example. Though he was a slave in Egypt, he became steward over Potiphar's house. That Egyptian master "left everything he owned in Joseph's charge" (Gen. 39:6). It was Joseph's responsibility to manage that household well, to not squander the family's resources but to improve them. Likewise, when Joseph rose to power in Egypt, he appointed a steward over his own house (44:4).

Typically, a steward's charge was a household or a large estate.[5] A steward was basically a housekeeper or estate manager. There are actually at least seventeen different Greek words related to the concept of household and household management used in the Bible.[6] But the basic principle is the same. And a household manager was held accountable to the master of the estate for how he discharged his administration.[7]

Wealthy landowners used stewards to manage the affairs of their land, houses, or businesses. A steward could be a trusted employee or a son, but most often was a slave.[8] This was also true in Old Testament times. The Septuagint (the Greek translation of the Old Testament) also used *oikonomos* to refer to "a kind of chief slave who superintended the household and even the whole property of his master."[9] And in Luke 12:42–43 "steward" was used interchangeably with servant or slave *(doulos).* So, it seems safe to say that stewards and slaves were closely related. And in our parable, though the men were never called stewards, only slaves, they fit the description of stewards. But what did stewards do in their household management?

---

5   Ruth Ann Foster. "Stewardship: Sign and Substance of the Christian Life as Taught in the New Testament." *Southwestern Journal of Theology,* Vol. 37, no. 2 (1995), 15.

6   William L. Hendericks, "Stewardship in the New Testament." *Southwestern Journal of Theology*, Vol. 13, No. 2, 25–28.

7   William L. Hendericks., 27; *Theological Dictionary of the New Testament 5:119–56.*

8   W. Clyde Tilley, "A Biblical Approach to Stewardship." *Review & Expositor,* 84 (3): 433–42.

9   O. Michel, "οικονομος," *Theological Dictionary of the New Testament,* 5:148–50.

A steward's responsibilities could include accounting, estate management, inspection of goods, housekeeping, or overseeing the cooking. A steward may have been over an entire estate or given charge over some branch of the household.[10] Sometimes they would oversee the other slaves, a sort of "head slave" position. But at bottom, a steward was someone who didn't belong to themselves yet was entrusted with a great responsibility.

Stewards were quite often entrusted with more responsibility than even members of the master's own family. The bar for a steward's character, therefore, must have been quite high. After all, the master would leave this person alone with their most valuable assets.

STEWARDS OF THE KING

This is how the New Testament talks about Christians as well; we are slaves and stewards of the King of kings. Based on Jesus' teaching that His disciples were stewards, early Christians adopted this term to describe the spiritual responsibilities of the believer toward God.[11] Paul picked up on the way Jesus applied the terms of stewardship in the parables and expanded on them in His epistles.[12] He said ministers of the gospel should be regarded as both stewards (oikonomia) and servants (1 Cor. 4:1–2). First Peter 4:10 applied the concept of stewardship to Christians exercising their spiritual gifts "as good stewards of the manifold grace of God." An elder in a church was likewise called "God's steward" (Titus 1:7).[13] And other stewardship terms like "entrusted" were similarly applied to believers (Luke 12:48; 16:11; Gal. 2:7; 1 Thess. 2:4; 1 Tim. 1:18; 6:20; 2 Tim. 2:2).

But the New Testament application of *oikonomia* goes even further than this. Stewardship was used as a metaphor to describe not just the believer's responsibility to God but also God's own plan and administration of salvation (Eph. 1:10; 3:9). In the same way that a servant would partner with a master to administer the master's plans and economy concerning an estate, we have the immense privilege of partnering with God in His economy of salvation for the ages. In this sense we become "stewards of the mysteries of God" (1 Cor. 4:1). Or as one author put it, our stewardship becomes

10 O. Michel, "οικονομος," *Theological Dictionary of the New Testament*, 5:148–50.

11 W. Clyde Tilley, "A Biblical Approach to Stewardship."

12 *Theological Dictionary of the New Testament*, 5:148–51.

13 Ruth Ann Foster, "Stewardship: Sign and Substance of the Christian Life as Taught in the New Testament." *Southwestern Journal of Theology*, 37, no. 2 (1995), 15.

"partnership with Christ, through the Holy Spirit, in fulfilling the purpose of God in the world."[14]

It quickly becomes apparent that New Testament stewardship encompasses far more than responsibility for only financial or material resources. Stewardship in the Christian sense "includes our time, talents, and self as well as possessions and so embraces the Christian's responsibility to God for one's total existence."[15] Christian stewardship is life stewardship.

Recognizing this great and humbling honor, we should next ask, "What qualities make a good steward?" What can we learn from ancient stewards that will show us the characteristics of faithfulness we might seek to cultivate in our own stewardship before God?

Finding a Quality Steward

The reason wealthy landowners in Jesus' day used stewards was because they often lived in cities that were far from their agricultural properties. Naturally, they needed to appoint stewards to oversee the laborers and day-to-day necessities of managing those estates.[16] But instead of hiring an outsider for this position, stewards in the Roman world were almost always "promoted from within." A slave who had proved himself trustworthy would receive the honor of a larger stewardship and the other benefits that attended this position.

A master would not want to entrust just anyone with overseeing the estate. He would have had an extensive vetting process. Like the master in the parable of the talents, he had to be able to trust these stewards not to steal, squander, or take advantage of their position, especially in his absence. Stewards had to be people of a certain character.

In the first century, the Roman writer Lucius Inuits Moderatus Columella (c. ad 70) penned a series of twelve books on agriculture, titled De Re Rustica, "On Rural Affairs." In this work, Columella advised masters on the qualities to look for in steward. He said a good steward should be "one who [had] been tested by experience." And he would have "such qualities of feeling that he [would] exercise authority without laxness and without cruelty." And finally, "This above all else is required of him—that he shall not think

---

14 A. C. Conrad, *The Divine Economy: A Study in Stewardship* (Grand Rapids: Wm. B. Eerdmans, 1954), 27.

15 W. Clyde Tilley, "A Biblical Approach to Stewardship."

16 This is the backdrop of the parable of the tenants in Matt. 21:33–46.

that he knows what he does not know, and that he shall always be eager to learn.[17] It's remarkable how so many of these qualities come through in the example of the faithful stewards in the parable of the talents.

In the parable of the talents, we find that the two faithful stewards share certain character qualities. A careful reading of Matthew 25:16–18 is instructive for knowing the qualities that Jesus Himself said made for a faithful steward. We should pay close attention here, because these character qualities are what we are called to cultivate in our own lives if we desire to be faithful stewards for Christ.

In Matthew 25:16–18 we see how the three stewards handled their various charges:

> Immediately the one who had received the five talents went and traded with them, and he gained five more talents. In the same manner the one who *had received* the two *talents* gained two more. But he who had received the one *talent* went and dug *a hole* in the ground and hid his master's money.

The first two stewards traded with their talents and doubled the investment, whereas the third simply hid the money. For the purposes of our examination, the first two stewards we will call the responsible stewards, and the third steward with the one talent we will call the renegade steward.

CHARACTERISTICS OF A RESPONSIBLE STEWARD

In Matthe 25:16–17 we observe three characteristics of responsible stewards: *diligence, integrity*, and *godliness*. They are easily remembered by the acronym *DIG*. If we can develop these qualities in our own life stewardship, we are well on our way to carrying out our trust in a way that honors and pleases our Lord.

Diligence

The first quality of faithful stewardship is diligence. Notice how the first two stewards were industrious. Matthew 25:16 says the first steward "immediately" went and traded. He did not delay to obey. He was proactively faithful, seeking ways to best use his master's resources. Diligent stewards are like Abraham who, when commanded to sacrifice Isaac, instead of arguing or looking for excuses, trusted God and rose early in the morning to

---

17 "De re rustica" (English translation), Loeb Classical Library edition, 1941, http://penelope.uchicago.edu/Thayer/E/Roman/Texts/Varro/de_Re_Rustica/home.html (accessed October 28, 2022).

obey (Gen. 22:3). Diligent stewards set about their work quickly. They do not waste time. This rapid obedience contrasts with the renegade steward whom the master calls wicked and lazy (Matt. 25:26).

Too often we are slow in our duties. We say we want to serve God, but when opportunity arises, we take our sweet time. However, delayed obedience is disobedience. Just look at the story of Jonah, a prophet who, when called by God to preach repentance to the Ninevites, did everything in his power to delay and run from obeying that command (Jon. 1).

Even in the laying down of the Law of Moses, God frequently noted that obedience was to be prompt. "You shall not delay *the offering from* your harvest and your vintage" (Exod. 22:29). Likewise, the people of Israel were instructed that delaying to fulfill any promise they made to Lord was the same as if they had sinned: "When you make a vow to the LORD your God, you shall not delay to pay it, for it would be sin in you, and the LORD your God will surely require it of you" (Deut. 23:21). Responsible stewards, therefore, must be diligent and not delay to fulfill their duty.

Diligent stewards also act wisely with their stewardship because they know it does not belong to them. Randy Alcorn says it well,

> Because they are managing the master's assets, servants must choose their investments carefully. They can neither afford to take undue risks nor let capital erode through idleness. The goal isn't merely to conserve resources but to multiply them. The servants must be intelligent, resourceful, and strategic thinkers regarding the best long-term investments.[18]

We must be sure to not make poor investments with Jesus' resources. And, again, this includes all that we've been called to steward. We must be wise with our finances, work, skills, opportunities, relationships, and time. We must treat every job opportunity like an investment and every skill we possess like a card to be wisely played. It's not ours to squander on a bad bet. Our job is to deploy the Master's resources for maximum returns. So faithful stewards are marked by diligence.

Integrity

The second quality of a responsible steward is integrity. This just means that faithful servants of Christ keep their word. Both the parable of the ten minas and the parable of the talents start the same way: The master leaves on a journey (Matt. 25:14; Luke 19:12). When the boss is away there is always a temptation to slack off. But Christians are to be honest in all our dealings,

---

18   Randy Alcorn, *Money, Possessions and Eternity,* 148.

even when no one is watching. We must always remember that we serve at the pleasure of the Master, and He will return to settle accounts.

Just as an ancient master had to be sure his stewards were people of honest character, in the same way, integrity is another prerequisite for responsible stewardship. It's tempting to cut corners in our work when no one is around. But when we take seriously that our whole lives are a stewardship, we will respect the Master enough to be honest because we are representing Him. This means not slacking at our jobs, not being sneaky about wasting time, and not hiding when we make mistakes.

Practically, we must keep short accounts with God. We must confess our sins as soon as we are aware of them. And we must not search out excuses for our poor stewardship. It's all about honesty. Because a responsible steward is marked by integrity.

Godliness

The third quality of a responsible steward is godliness. Despite how little instruction these stewards were given, the first two knew exactly what to do. How did they know? It is surprising how little information the master gave them about how to invest his talents. Nevertheless, he rightfully expected them to know what to do. That's because faithful stewards know their master well enough to know what he would want them to do.

An ancient steward would have spent a lot of time training with the master to understand the way he wanted his estate operated. The faithful stewards would have been attentive to the master's behavior, noting each decision, seeking to understand the way he thought. After a while they would begin to behave and think just like the master. So the master could reasonably expect that while he was away his stewards would make choices he would have made were he there. "A pupil is not above his teacher; but everyone, after he has been fully trained, will be like his teacher" (Luke 6:40).

When I spend more than a few days with someone who has an accent, I find that I start to talk like him or her. This can be a little embarrassing, because that one can think I'm mocking him. But when you spend a lot of time with someone you start to act like that person. And the better you know someone, the more easily you can anticipate their expectations and desires. When you spend more time with God, you think and act more like God. This is the quality Christians call godliness.

Godliness is a virtue that is praised throughout the New Testament (1 Tim. 2:10; 3:16; 4:7, 8; 5:4; 6:3–11; 2 Tim. 3:5; Titus 1:1; 2 Pet. 1:3–7;

3:11). Godliness simply means to be like God. A godly person is someone who images the character of God in their life. But it's only possible to be godly if you walk with God. And this is a crucial quality of a good steward.

We are better able to serve Jesus in how we invest our time, talents, and treasure when we walk with Him daily. By being disciplined to read the Word daily and pray, we train ourselves to think His thoughts after Him. We are learning to instinctively know what pleases God.

If your aim is to please God, then you'll want to be a responsible steward. And if you want to be a responsible steward you should work to develop in diligence, integrity, and godliness. These are the qualities we see in the two faithful stewards in this parable. But the third steward was a different story. We can also learn from his stewardship, but only as a cautionary tale.

Characteristics of a Renegade Steward

Our culture worships rebels, renegades, and rogues. In the celebrities it elevates, the heroes it admires, and the stories it tells, our culture constantly praises those who buck authority and "stick it to the man." But rebellion should never be found in a Christian's heart.

Rebellion is the opposite of stewardship. Stewards, after all, are first slaves. They are submitted to the authority of their master. Many in our culture would hold up the third steward in the parable of the talents as someone to be praised. However, in Jesus' story, he is instead held up as an example of the attitudes a faithful steward must avoid.

After the faithful stewards invested what had been entrusted to them, the parable described what the third steward did with his portion, "But he who received the one *talent* went away and dug *a hole* in the ground and hid his master's money" (Matt. 25:18).

Unlike the first two stewards, who invested the talents the master entrusted to them with diligence, integrity, and godliness, this third steward simply buried his portion in the ground (see also Luke 19:20–21).

I remember hearing this parable when I was a child and feeling bad for the third steward because, as we'll see, when the master returned, this steward was condemned for burying the master's money. Was his behavior really that bad?

It doesn't seem like such a big deal to bury the money, does it? It's not like he stole it or lost it. But when you compare the third steward to the first two, we see that he was marked by the opposite qualities than those that define a faithful steward. Whereas the first two stewards had *diligence, integrity*, and *godliness*, the third steward was *disloyal, obstinate,* and *gutless.* Instead of the *DIG* acronym, think *DOG.*

Disloyal

The third steward was not condemned merely because he buried the money in the ground instead of investing it. *Why* he buried the money was the real problem for the master. It turned out that this steward hated the master. He was disloyal. We see his low view of the master come out when he explained to the master what he did with the talent.

> And the one also who had received the one talent came up and said, "Master, I knew you to be a hard man, reaping where you did not sow and gathering where you scattered no *seed.* And I was afraid, and went away and hid your talent in the ground. See, you have what is yours." (Matt. 25:24–25)

Don't be deceived. This is no innocent admission of fear. And it's not a harmless excuse. This response is not worthy of our pity. His explanation was an attack on the master's character. He revealed that his motivation for not making good use of the talent was his low view of the master.

The disloyalty of the faithless steward was made even more apparent in the parable of the ten minas, because that parable included commentary on how the renegade stewards viewed the master. The reason they were disloyal in their stewardship was because they outright hated the master and his rule.

> And he called ten of his slaves, and gave them ten minas, and said to them, "Do business *with this* until I come *back.*" But his citizens hated him and sent a delegation after him, saying, "We do not want this man to reign over us." (Luke 19:13–14)

Our failure to steward God's gifts faithfully cannot be explained away by laziness alone. Instead, our lack of motivation may indicate a lack of loyalty. A loyal steward is a faithful steward. When you care enough about something you find the motivation to do it. A faithful steward will make the most of whatever Christ has entrusted to her. Because He is her Lord, and she loves Him.

Too often we are tempted to focus on our rights instead of our responsibilities. We think it's not fair, so we complain at the lot God has assigned to us. We should be wary when we start thinking this way, for that is the behavior of the renegade steward. Instead of taking responsibility, he shifted blame. We must always remember that:

As stewards our rights are limited by our lack of ownership. Instead, we manage assets for the owner's benefit, and we carry no sense of entitlement to the assets we manage. It's our job to find out what the owner wants done with his assets, then carry out his will.[19]

When we start focusing on what we think we deserve instead of on what our master requires of us, we lose a proper perspective and enter spiritually dangerous territory.

Obstinate

The second mark of the renegade steward was that he was obstinate. He stubbornly refused to do what he was told. He knew what the master wanted him to do with the money, but he decided to stick it to him instead. He knew he couldn't simply steal the money or give it away without facing severe consequences. So his rebellious heart did the next best thing—he stubbornly decided to not improve the talent.

Really, this is a matter of trust. This steward admitted that he did not believe the master was good or a rewarder of faithfulness. He accused the master of being someone who reaped where he did not sow and gathered where he didn't plant seed (Matt. 25:24). So, in his contempt for the master, he scorned his responsibility for investing what was entrusted to him.

Christian stewardship is a matter of faith. And part of faith is believing that God rewards faithfulness. As Hebrews 11:6 says, "And without faith it is impossible to please *Him,* for he who comes to God must believe that He is and *that* He is a rewarder of those who seek Him." Belief in God is not the bare belief that God exists, but also belief that He has done and will do what He promises. We'll talk more about how this important factor of motivation and reward relates to stewardship in the next chapter. Because unlike the renegade steward, those who believe God fulfills His promises are not obstinate in their obedience, they are eager.

Gutless

Finally, the third steward was not just disloyal and obstinate, he was also gutless. Instead of taking responsibility, he made excuses. He blamed the master for his own disloyalty. He was a coward. A faithful steward doesn't make excuses when he is unfaithful.

The same goes for us. When we Christians inevitably fail in our task of stewardship, we return to the Master with hat in hand and ask for forgiveness.

---

19   Randy Alcorn, *Money, Possessions and Eternity,* 149.

We then discover that He is gracious toward the contrite. Because "GOD IS OP-POSED TO THE PROUD, BUT GIVES GRACE TO THE HUMBLE" (James 4:6). Those who have known the grace of God have no cause for fear, no matter how great their failures.

CONCLUSION

God does not apportion to all of us the same talents, but He has the same expectations for our character. He wants stewards who are diligent, have integrity, and are godly. But He opposes those who are disloyal, obstinate, and gutless in their stewardship.

As you await Christ's return, what kind of steward will you choose to be while the Master is away? Because, make no mistake, upon the Master's return there will be an accounting. In the next chapter, we will turn our attention to the reward for faithful stewardship.

Study Questions:

1. Why does it matter that Christians view themselves as slaves of God?

2. What were the differences between a steward and a slave in the ancient world?

3. What character qualities of a righteous steward do you think you already embody well? Which ones are you lacking?

4. Have you ever felt bad for the third servant? Why was what he did so bad and unacceptable?

5. What are some ways in which you can walk closer with Jesus so you can learn to be a better steward of what He has entrusted to you?

5

The Compensation of Stewardship

Now after a long time the master of those
slaves came and settled accounts with them.

Matthew 25:19

MANY OF OUR FAVORITE movies end with scenes of an award ceremony. Think of the final scene of *Star Wars: A New Hope* when everyone receives his or her medal or the heartwarming conclusion of Pixar's *Up* when the little boy, Russell, finally gets his merit badge. There is something so satisfying about seeing good deeds being rewarded. The reason we love it in stories is because we long for that kind of recognition in our own lives as well.

I've never been very good at basketball. But I did receive an award at the end of my seventh-grade basketball season. The coach gave me a little plastic trophy that said, "Most Improved." I remember how proud I felt. I had worked hard, stayed late after every practice, and hustled in every game. I knew I wasn't the best, but I felt proud to know my efforts had been noticed and rewarded.

The truth is, God has wired us for reward. And as we'll see from the last part of the parable of the talents, an eternal compensation awaits believers who persist in faithful stewardship until the end.

In Matthew 25:19–30, the master in the parable recompensed the servants according to their faithfulness. And this scene is a call to believers to be eternally minded as we approach own stewardship. It's also an affirmation that heavenly reward is a right and proper motivation for obedience and effort in the Christian life.

Let's look at what this reward is, the principles by which the master assessed faithfulness, and how Christ intends us to apply this part of the parable to how we steward our lives.

The Master's Return

In Matthew 25:19 the master returned from his journey, and he discovered how the stewards had used the talents he left them: "Now after a long time the master of those slaves came and settled accounts with them."

This return is symbolic of Christs' second coming and subsequent judgment. Christ's return will be a time of both judgment and reward. "The nations were enraged, and Your wrath came, and the time *came* for the dead to be judged, and *the time* to reward your bond-servants the prophets and the saints and those who fear Your name, the small and the great, and to destroy those who destroy the earth" (Rev. 11:18).

Often when we hear the word "judgment" we think only of negative judgment: wrath, punishment, and shame. And indeed, that is what judgment will entail for those who have not bowed the knee to Christ. But for those who have put their faith in Jesus, judgment day is a day for us to look forward to.

Look again at Revelation 11:18. It says it will be a time of judgment and reward. Likewise, the apostle Paul said of the coming judgment, "Then each man's praise will come to him from God" (1 Cor. 4:5). There are two sides to judgment: wrath and reward.

In this parable, we see both sides clearly. And without apology, Jesus holds out reward as a worthy motivation for a steward. But this part of the parable can be disorienting for Protestant Christians who affirm that justification is by faith alone.

We can sometimes find it bewildering to see good works rewarded in the New Testament. After all, isn't salvation by grace alone, through faith alone and not according to our works?

I want to show you from these verses why eternal reward for our faithfulness is not at odds with the free gift of salvation, and why embracing reward as a motivation will make you a better steward of your life and ultimately bring more glory to God. Then we will see how the wrath side of judgment plays out for the unfaithful steward, and what we can learn from that.

Reward for the Faithful Stewardship

Let's look at the reward side of the equation first. After the master returned, he settled accounts with the first two stewards. And he rewarded them according to their faithfulness. Both the steward with five talents and the one with two were commended because both doubled their investment.

The one who had received the five talents came and brought five more talents, saying, "Master, you entrusted five talents to me. See, I have gained five more talents." His master said to him, "Well done, good and faithful slave. You were faithful with a few things, I will put you in charge of many things; enter into the joy of your master" (Matt. 25:20–23).

This pattern is repeated for both stewards:

1. Presentation

2. Commendation

3. Promotion

4. Invitation

The steward comes forward, presenting his work to the master and saying, "Master, you delivered to me x talents; here I have made x talents more." The master responded with a commendation, "Well done, good and faithful slave." And then adds a promotion, "You were faithful with a few things, I will put you in charge of many things." But he doesn't stop there; he concludes with an invitation, "Enter into the joy of your master."

As we saw in Chapter 2, the talents represent all that God has entrusted to us: our time, talents, and treasure. These are the trust we've been called to steward until Christ returns. The point of this parable is that faithfulness in that task will be met with reward when Christ comes back. We will present to Him what we've done, receive a commendation, be rewarded with a promotion over more responsibilities in heaven, and be invited into the fullness of eternal life with Jesus.

Let's dig a bit deeper into the exact nature of this heavenly reward. But before we do that, I want to address the elephant in the room. This sure sounds like Christians are being rewarded for good works. Isn't this contrary to the gospel?

THE RIGHTNESS OF THE REWARD

When the New Testament talks about laboring for heavenly reward, it can strike us as odd for two reasons. First, isn't the reward for the Christian simply eternal life in heaven? And isn't that reward secured by faith alone in Jesus Christ? So how can we say that our reward is in any way tied to our faithfulness? Wouldn't that be salvation by works?

Second, isn't it wrong to be motivated to do good because of the reward? That seems like a rather selfish way to look at obedience.

Let's first look at the place of reward for our works. It is true that salvation is by grace alone through faith alone. But Christians often overlook that there is more to eternal reward than just going to heaven. Ephesians 2:8–9 is one of the most succinct and clear declarations that salvation is purely by grace through faith and explicitly not a matter of our works.

> For by grace you have been saved through faith; and that not of yourselves, *it is* the gift of God, not as a result of works, so that no one may boast.

It couldn't be clearer: Works do not contribute to our salvation.

But then immediately after saying this, the apostle Paul went on to say that this salvation is, in fact, accompanied by good works that God preordained for us. "For we are His workmanship, created in Christ Jesus for good works, which God prepared beforehand so that we would walk in them" (Eph. 2:10).

Good works do not contribute to our salvation, but they do follow it. What's so incredible is that the New Testament tells us God actually rewards us for doing these good works He prepared in advance for us to walk in.

But the reward for our good works is not salvation—that is already secured by faith in Jesus Christ. Instead, our faithfulness as believers is rewarded with additional treasure in heaven. This is what the apostle Paul talked about in First Corinthians 3:10–15, when he spoke of building on the foundation of Jesus Christ:

> According to the grace of God which was given to me, like a wise master builder I laid a foundation, and another is building on it. But each man must be careful how he builds on it. For no man can lay a foundation other than the one which is laid, which is Jesus Christ. Now if any man builds on the foundation with gold, silver, precious stones, wood, hay, straw, each man's work will become evident, for the day will show it, because it is *to be* revealed with fire, and the fire itself will test the quality of each man's work. If any man's work which he has built on it remains, he will receive a reward. If any man's work is burned up, he will suffer loss; but he himself will be saved, yet so as through fire.

Some good works will follow every Christian's salvation. No believer is without any good works. But if you have placed your faith in Jesus Christ, your salvation is secure regardless of the how many good works may follow. The foundation is laid. But we build on that with good works which will be "revealed with fire" that "will test the quality of each man's work." That's a reference to judgment. And "If any man's work which he has built on it remains, he will receive a reward." But if any Christian's works don't survive the judgment, "he will suffer loss; but he himself will be saved."

Notice it's not that the good works contribute to your salvation or that a lack of good works can cause you to lose your salvation. Salvation is not the issue in question. This is about an eternal reward ceremony in which Jesus will recompense Christians according to their good works.

Throughout the New Testament reward is promised as a strong motivation for living faithful lives before Christ.

Take Matthew 6:19–21, for example. Jesus cautioned His disciples about laying up treasure on earth, "Do not store up for yourselves treasures on earth." Why? Because treasure here is temporal, it will not last.

Earthly treasure is subject to destruction by "moth and rust" or theft from those would "break in and steal." Instead, Jesus told them, "Store up for yourselves treasures in heaven, where neither moth nor rust destroys, and where thieves do not break in or steal; for where your treasure is, there your heart will be also."

He didn't tell them, "Be good for goodness' sake." That's Santa Claus's line. No, Jesus told the disciples that the good they did in this life would be rewarded. Notice he didn't rush to say, "But that's not why you should do it!" His whole point was that the sacrifices we make with regard to temporal treasures will be well worth it, because there is a permanent reward for faithfulness in heaven. Eternal reward is a good motivation.

I'm saddened that this has been underemphasized in the modern church because it is such a powerful motivation.

The reason I can give away my money instead of spending it on myself, invest my time volunteering instead of vegging on the couch, or use my unique talents to serve the church instead of my own interests—and do those things joyfully—isn't because the giving is its own reward. It's because I serve a promise-keeping God who said He will recompense faithful stewardship. I'm not being a fool by storing my treasure in heaven, I'm following the wisest investment strategy ever.

It certainly does feel good to give, but when Paul quoted Jesus to the Ephesian elders as saying, "It is more blessed to give than to receive" (Acts 20:35), he wasn't using that expression in the same way we so often do. He wasn't saying "It's better to give because it makes you feel nice inside." That may look cute on a cross-stitch, but it guts the phrase of all its meaning. Jesus literally meant you will be more blessed by giving than receiving, eternally speaking. There will be a reward for generosity.

The modern church has gutted Christians of the very incentives God designed to motivate our obedient stewardship. When we insist that obedience should always be done without a view to the reward, we are saying something that sounds pious but runs counter to Scripture and God's design for how human beings are motivated.

Randy Alcorn points out how wrong this view of incentive-less obedience really is:

> Most of us use rewards to motivate our children. So why are we surprised that God uses rewards to motivate us? By God's own design, all of us need incentives to motivate us to do our jobs and do them well. Motivation by reward is not a result of the fall, but God's original design for humanity. To say, "I don't do anything for the reward—I do it only because it's right," may appear to take the spiritual high road. But in fact it's pseudospiritual. It goes against the grain of the way God created us and the way he tries to motivate us.[1]

The Scriptures speak plainly on this matter. Take, for example, Ephesians 6:8 which says we are to do our work not for the praise of men, but for the praise of God "knowing that whatever good thing each one does, this he will receive back from the Lord" (Eph. 6:8). Or see Romans 2:6 which says, "[God] will render to each person according to his deeds." And the reward will be "glory and honor and peace to everyone who does good" (2:10). Here are just a few areas of obedience which the Scriptures say we will receive rewards for:

- Self-denial (Matt. 16:24–27)
- Compassion for the needy (Luke 14:13–14)
- Loving our enemies (Luke 6:35)
- Generosity (Matt. 19:21)
- Enduring hardship and persecution in faith (Heb. 10:34–36; Luke 6:22–23)

All throughout the New Testament, eternal reward for good works is held out as a positive motivation for serving Christ and living a godly life (2 Pet. 3:11–14). To obey with a view to eternal reward is not some lesser, selfish motive. In fact, it is the very nature of faith to seek God for the reward that He promises. Hebrews 11:6 says that whoever would come after God must believe that He rewards. For what is faith but trust? And what is trust but believing the words of the one you trust are true?

---

1   Randy Alcorn, *Money, Possessions and Eternity*, 130.

When we are motivated to obedience for the sake of reward, we are honoring God because we are believing His promises. We walk by faith in the promises of God, and God promises reward.

So, this isn't talking about earning your salvation, and this is not a mercenary motive. The parable illustrates that God will reward faithful stewardship. Specifically, this part of the parable is not talking about the judgment unto salvation, which all mankind will face and be judged based on whether they trusted Christ or not. Instead, it is talking about the second judgment that is only for believers (2 Cor. 5:10; Rom. 14:10, 12). And this second judgment is all about reward for faithfulness.

We should note that our ability to do these good works that please God and result in our reward is also a gift of grace. As one author put it,

> Whatever reward may accrue to servants of Christ is not from anyone's ability to autonomously earn a reward; even rewards come from God's grace. Our ability to do good works is a gift. Nevertheless, rewards will be consistent with our actions. Our daily actions matter, both now and in eternity.[2]

The only reason anyone can be a faithful steward is because "It is God who is at work in you, both to will and to work for *His* good pleasure" (Phil. 2:13). Our next question might be: "If it's not salvation, then what exactly is this reward?"

THE NATURE OF THE REWARD

It's one thing to say, "heavenly reward," but that sounds nebulous. What are we talking about here, a bigger harp? Here again the parable packs a lot of information into very few words.

With both faithful stewards, the master's response followed the same pattern. After their presentation they received his commendation, "Well done, good and faithful slave"; a promotion, "You were faithful with a few things, I will put you in charge of many things"; and an invitation, "Enter into the joy of your master'" (Matt. 25:20–23). Let's look at these three aspects of the reward: commendation, promotion, and invitation.

Commendation

First there is a commendation. He tells them "Well done, good and faithful slave." Can you think of a higher honor than to be patted on the back by

---

2 Brandon D. Crowe, *Every Day Matters: A Biblical Approach to Productivity* (Bellingham, WA: Lexham Press, 2020), 32.

the master you love to serve and to be told "You did well. You were faithful." I've had friends who never heard their earthly fathers say, "I'm proud of you." The absence of fatherly praise wreaked emotional havoc in many of their lives far into adulthood.

We were created to crave the affirmation of the authority figures in our lives. Every desire to hear "Well done" from a parent, coach, teacher, mentor, or boss is a faint echo of the deeper longing God put in our hearts to hear "Well done" from the Master Himself.

All of life is a quest for glory—we want to give glory to a worthy object and receive it from the same. We love to see glory in athletes, celebrities, or other accomplished people. And we love to receive glory through the praise from those we respect.

Have you ever fantasized about meeting someone you deeply admire? We imagine what we might say, but we also dream about what they might say to us. We want the people we are impressed by to be impressed by us.

The trouble is that we often look for glory in all the wrong places. In high school, we are drawn to certain peer groups; we hold up their style, their attitudes, and their opinions as our standard. We dress a certain way, act a certain way, feign interest in certain topics so we might be perceived as part of their group.

We want to receive glory from those whom we deem glorious. This desire for glory is normal, but it is misdirected. The object we were made to find most glorious is God Himself. For He is the being who is most glorious and worthy of our admiration and praise. And we were created to desire the affirmation that can only come from God. It's baked into our design as image bearers.

Success in image bearing is to look as much like the One in whose image we were fashioned and to be commended for it. There is a reason my son beams from ear-to-ear when his mom tells him, "You look just like daddy!"

The prize of being honored by God is worth all the sufferings of this life. In Romans, the apostle Paul said the believer who persisted in the faith would be glorified with Christ "if indeed we suffer with *Him* so that we may also be glorified with *Him*" (Rom. 8:17).

This is such a powerful motivation that he added that he considered "that the sufferings of this present time are not worthy to be compared with the glory that is to be revealed to us" (8:18). Similarly, Paul spoke of "an eternal weight of glory far beyond all comparison" that awaits us on the other side of the sufferings of this life (2 Cor. 4:17).

C.S. Lewis argued that this weight of glory we are awaiting is the commendation of Jesus Christ. It is that "Well done good and faithful slave," from the parable of the talents.[3]

What a joyous day to look forward to, when our Lord who loved us and gave Himself for us that we might be redeemed looks on our lives with the smile of approval and says, "Well done!" That is a reward well worth laboring for. But amazingly commendation is just one part of the prize for faithful stewardship.

Promotion

Second, we see the master not only commended the servants, but He also promised them another reward as well. He said, "You were faithful with a few things, I will put you in charge of many things" (Matt. 25:21).

Because the stewards were trustworthy with the talents entrusted to them, the master promised an even greater trust. Likewise, we can expect a greater trust in heaven if we are faithful with our time, talents, and treasure.

Several years ago, I was talking to someone about how God will entrust us with more responsibility in heaven based on how responsible we are in this life. He said that he didn't think more responsibility sounded like much of a reward. We've been trained by our culture to see responsibility as a burden to be avoided, as more of an inconvenience than an honor.

But being given more responsibility is an incredible reward. It's a promotion. It's an honor. Like when your boss recognizes a job well done and promotes you to oversee a greater portion of the company. Or when you have a great soccer season, and the coach promotes you to captain. Or like when you were a kid and you proved you were responsible with your chores, so your parents let you get a dog. Being given greater responsibility is an honor. For the slave of Christ, whose chief aim is to serve and glorify the Master, being given more responsibility is the highest honor we could receive.

Consider promotion in kingdom terms. This is what Jesus is talking about here. In the parable of the ten minas, which closely parallels the parable of the talents, the master rewarded the servants by giving them rule over cities.

> And he said to him, "Well done, good slave, because you have been faithful in a very little thing, you are to be in authority over ten cities." The second came, saying, "Your mina, master, has made five minas." And he said to him also, "And you are to be over five cities" (Luke 19:17–19).

---

3 C. S. Lewis, *The Weight of Glory*, (San Francisco: HarperOne, 2009).

But this is not merely a metaphor. The Bible promises that faithful believers will be rewarded with literal promotions to rule over cities on the new earth. The reward for kingdom stewardship is that we will get to share in the rule of the Kingdom. This was promised way back in Daniel 7:27, which says, "Then the sovereignty, the dominion and the greatness of *all* the kingdoms under the whole heaven will be given to the people of the saints of the Highest One" (Dan. 7:27). Revelation 2:25–26 speaks of believers being given authority over nations. Revelation 5:9–10 says we will reign upon the earth. And in the parable of the talents the master told the faithful stewards "I will put you in charge of many things" (Matt. 25:21, 23).

This promise of promotion for faithfulness becomes even more obvious when you start to realize that all of the "crowns" promised to believers (1 Cor. 9:24–25; 1 Thess. 2:19; 2 Tim. 4:8; 1 Pet. 5:4; Rev. 2:10) aren't just fancy headwear but representations of rulership.

Who wears crowns? Kings and princes. When our Master returns from His journey, He will promote us to rule with Him in His kingdom in proportion to our faithfulness.

This should come as no surprise. Remember, God's plan from the beginning was that mankind would rule over creation. Throughout the story of redemption, the restoration of this original order has always been part of God's plan. He has always been seeking to make "a kingdom of priests" (Exod. 19:6; Isa. 61:6; 1 Pet. 2:9; Rev. 1:6).

You will receive additional honor and responsibility in heaven based on your faithfulness to steward what God has given you in this life. And these responsibilities are essentially more opportunities to honor and serve the God you love.

What an incredible thing to look forward to! What a great reason to not slacken our pace! But as if that weren't amazing enough, there is still one more aspect to the reward.

Invitation

Third, the master not only rewarded with a commendation and a promotion, but he also included an invitation to "Enter the joy of your master" (Matt. 25:21, 23). In the parable, this is perhaps the master inviting his faithful stewards to a feast of celebration or perhaps a coda to his announcement of their promotion to fuller members of his estate.

The thrust of the invitation is that little word, "joy." Jesus was saying the ultimate reward for Christians is not just the commendation or promotion, but that we will participate in the joy of our Lord. He was talking about our being with Him, the One in whose "presence is fullness of joy" and in whose "right hand there are pleasures forevermore" (Ps. 16:11).

Even as I write these words, my heart fills with excitement. Is there any greater hope, any greater motivation, any greater reason to jump out of bed in the morning and commit yourself to serving God? Do you long for the joy of the Lord? Is your stewardship of this life driven by that quest for commendation, promotion, and invitation to eternal joy? Doesn't it make you want to seize every moment, steward every dollar, and exploit every opportunity in service of the Lord?

THE PROPORTIONALITY OF THE REWARD

In this part of the parable, we must not miss the proportionality of the reward. The second servant was entrusted with less and earned a smaller reward from the master than the first. He was given two talents and earned two more, while the first servant was entrusted with five and earned five more. Yet, they both received the same reward. The language in Matthew 25:21 and 25:23 was identical. What are we to learn from this? This principal: God rewards in proportion to our faithfulness, not in proportion to what He entrusts to us.

It is easy to evaluate your stewardship in light of what other have been entrusted with. We start comparing our talents with others and can quickly feel jealous. But whether you have been entrusted with gifts great or small, your mission is still the same: Be faithful. And you can trust that He who rewards will reward rightly and abundantly on the last day, not according to what you were given but according to how faithful you were it.

THE MASTER'S WRATH

Now we must turn to the other side of the judgment coin, from reward to wrath. For the final steward in the parable was unfaithful and disloyal to the master. His fate was not commendation, promotion, or invitation. Rather, he was cast into outer darkness.

> And the one also who had received the one talent came up and said, "Master, I knew you to be a hard man, reaping where you did not sow and gathering where you scattered no *seed*. And I was afraid, and went away and hid your talent in the ground. See, you have what is yours." But his master answered and said to him, "You wicked, lazy slave, you knew that I reap where I did not sown and gather where I scattered no *seed*. Then you ought to have put

my money in the bank, and on my arrival I would have received my *money* back with interest. Therefore take away the talent from him, and give it to the one who has the ten talents. For to everyone who has, *more* shall be given, and he will have an abundance; but from the one who does not have, even what he does have shall be taken away. Throw out the worthless slave into the outer darkness; in that place there will be weeping and gnashing of teeth." (Matt. 25:24–30)

As we've already noted, the third servant revealed his view of the master when confronted. Instead of owning his failure to steward what was entrusted to him, he accused the master of being a harsh and thieving man.

So, it is with all who refuse to submit to Jesus as Lord. I've heard that the two tenants of atheism are "God doesn't exist, and I hate Him."

Unbelief is not a neutral position. Those who refuse to serve God don't do so because they are indifferent, but because they hate Him.

But sometimes God-haters can fly under the radar for a long time. Psalm 81:15 speaks of those who "pretend obedience" to God, but ultimately will be found out and punished. That's what happened to the third steward. He did not even do the bare minimum to try to steward the master's talent.

So the master did two things. First, he took the talent from him and gave it to the steward who already had ten. Second, he cast the man into outer darkness.

What does all this mean for our life stewardship as Christians?

First, it makes sense that the master took the talent from the steward. But it seemed odd that the master gave the talent to the servant who already had the most. Jesus even inserted a bit of commentary here that shows something we should learn about kingdom economics from this exchange. He said, "For to everyone who has, *more* shall be given, and he will have an abundance; but from the one who does not have, even what he does have shall be taken away" (Matt. 25:29).

How are we to understand this principle that sounds unfair?

It's just reinforcing the principle that faithful stewardship is rewarded and rewarded abundantly.

"For to everyone who has" refers to the stewards who were faithful and increased their trust as a result. They had talents because they faithfully grew what was given to them.

"More shall be given," is again a restatement of something Jesus said many times before: When we are faithful with a little, we receive more (Luke 16:10). "He will have an abundance," refers to the compounding nature of eternal investments. The faithful Christian life is one that compounds to more and more trust and fruitfulness.

Jesus alluded to this principle in Matthew 13:8 when He spoke about the fruitfulness of the seed which fell on the good soil that produce a crop "some a hundredfold, some sixty, and some thirty." And He spoke of the same principal when He said those who would abide in Him would "bear much fruit" (John 15:5).

The last statement, "The one who does not have, even what he does have shall be taken away," refers to those whose lives bear no fruit. By their complete failure of stewardship, these people prove themselves to be unbelievers. Just as the unfaithful servant revealed that he did not trust the master, so those who claim the name of Christ but whose lives produce nothing godly demonstrate that they have not trusted in Jesus.

We have understood the first two servants as not having earned their salvation through faithful stewardship, but as having increased their heavenly reward by it. So, it can be alarming to find that the third steward seemed to have lost his salvation by lack of stewardship. But is this really the case?

No, the third steward does not illustrate a true believer who has lost salvation through disobedience. That is impossible. For salvation is a gift of God, and He keeps to the end those who are being saved (Heb. 7:25). If you have put your faith in Jesus Christ, no one can snatch you from His hand (John 10:28). The third steward in this parable did not represent a believer who has lost his faith, but someone who proved himself never to have had genuine faith. His lack of faithfulness evidenced a heart of faithlessness.

When pressed by the master, the third steward showed his true colors. We get a glimpse into his wicked heart.

Faithless stewards are not just lazy, they hate the master and do not regard him as their lord. This person is the wheat among the tares of Matthew 13:24–30, the goat among the sheep of Matthew 25:31–46. He represents a person who appears to be a member of Christ's church but is in fact a rebel in disguise.

Unbelievers will always be hidden among true believers. Sometimes these people reveal themselves through apostatizing. "They went out from us, but they were not *really* of us; for if they had been of us, they would have remained with us; but *they went out*, so that it would be shown that they all are not of us" (1 John 2:19).

Sometimes false believers can blend in until the very end. When the settling of accounts happens on the last day, however, they will be found out.

And though they may have enjoyed the blessings of the visible church for a time and shared in her gifts (Heb. 6:4), even that will be taken away (Matt. 25:28) and given to the true and faithful believers (25:29).

The end for this faithless steward, and indeed all who have not bowed the knee to Christ, was being cast into outer darkness where there was weeping and gnashing of teeth. This, of course, is a reference to hell.

This is a warning. Be sure that you have really trusted in Jesus Christ. Just being a member of a church is not enough, serving in the nursery is not enough, giving money is not enough, being a good person is not enough. A day of reckoning is coming when all will be revealed and both punishment and reward will be doled out.

CONCLUSION

For true believers this coming judgment is our great hope. It's the fuel in our tanks that motivates us to keep employing our gifts in the service of Christ and His church. We know when we do so, those gifts multiply. And we serve a God who is eager to reward our faithfulness with treasure in heaven and joys evermore.

Let us then learn the lesson of the parable of the talents. All Christ has entrusted to us—our talents, our money, our opportunities, our very lives—is a stewardship. It is all God's to be put to good use in the advancement of His kingdom. And on that day when He returns, we will find that any sacrifice we've made in His service will have been more than worth it. Because Jesus is a promise keeper and His words are true, "Everyone who has left houses or brothers or sisters or father or mother or children or farms for My name's sake, will receive many times as much, and will inherit eternal life" (19:29).

So let us labor hard, give generously, and steward well these lives for the glory of our great God!

Study Questions:

1. How does the reward promised for faithful stewardship differ from salvation and eternal life?

2. What do you think of heavenly reward as a motivation for obedient living? Does it still seem wrong to be motivated by that? Why or why not?

3. What lessons should we take from the way the righteous stewards were rewarded with commendation, promotion, and invitation?

4. Why did the third steward react as he did when the master confronted him about his lack of stewardship?

5. What are some things we can learn from the cautionary tale of the faithless steward?

PART 2

THE PRACTICE OF STEWARDSHIP

6

STEWARDING YOUR TIME

Making the most of your time, because the days are evil.

Ephesians 5:16

WE'VE CLOSELY EXAMINED the doctrine of stewardship from the Scriptures and specifically in the parable of the steward. Now it's time to get a little more practical. In these next three chapters we will look at principles and strategies that can help believers more faithfully steward their time, talents, and treasure.

Stewardship, as we have seen, encompasses all of life. But one facet of stewardship that is easy to overlook is that all stewardship must be done in time. What I mean is that every command of God, if it is to be obeyed, must be obeyed in time.

Every act of service, every choice, every investment, every relationship—all that we are responsible for managing before God must be performed in some specific place and some specific time. So, whether it's the stewardship of your spiritual resources or material ones, your success as a steward hinges on your ability to manage your time well.[1] So it's appropriate that the first practical area of life stewardship we explore is time.

When you start to view your life as a stewardship, this truth becomes painfully obvious: We don't have much time. With so many facets of life to steward, the question of how much time we commit to things like our work, relationships, and churches becomes a matter of urgent importance. So many of our hours each week go to our vocation, but are we spending that time well? Just because you are at the office from nine to five does not mean you are using each hour faithfully.

---

1   Parts of this chapter were adapted from my blog post, "Four Reasons Time Is Precious," Redeeming Productivity, https://redeemingproductivity.com/jonathan-edwards-4-reasons-time-is-precious/ (accessed Oct. 28, 2022).

Relationships also require time. As a friend of mine once quipped, "The most inefficient thing you can do is love." Paul even reminded us of how our service to the church is directly tied to our time and opportunities, "So then, while we have opportunity, let us do good to all people, and especially to those who are of the household of faith" (Gal. 6:10).

The scope of our stewardship is vast. We've been called to do so much, but have scarce time in which to do it all. That is why we must treat time itself like a talent to be stewarded.

So if we, with the Puritan Thomas Watson, recognize that "Time is a talent to trade with,"[2] how will we make the most of it? How do we steward our time well for the Master? Because like all of our talents, our time belongs to God, and He expects us to faithfully employ it for the good of others and His glory.

RECOGNIZE THE PRECIOUSNESS OF TIME

Some people say time is the most precious resource. Scriptures are not shy on this point. Several years ago, my own relationship with time was profoundly changed when I read a sermon by Jonathan Edwards entitled "The Preciousness of Time and the Importance of Redeeming It."

Dated December 1734, this short sermon pressed deep into Paul's injunction from Ephesians 5:16 to redeem the time. It left me, a man in my twenties, almost breathless with holy terror. I had never before slowed down long enough to consider the horrifying reality of just how brief my life really will be and how much of the Lord's time I had already squandered.

In the sermon, Edwards gave four reasons why time is precious. First, time is precious because eternity depends on it. "Gold and silver are esteemed precious by men; but they are of no worth to any man, only as thereby he has an opportunity of avoiding or removing some evil, or of possessing himself of some good."[3] But time is more precious than money because, "by it we have opportunity of escaping everlasting misery, and of obtaining everlasting blessedness and glory."[4]

---

2   Bobby Jamieson "Giving Time, Talents, and Treasures," *Tabletalk*, February 1, 2019, https://tabletalkmagazine.com/article/2019/02/giving-time-talents-treasures/ (accessed Oct. 28, 2022).

3   Jonathan Edwards, "The Preciousness Of Time And The Importance Of Redeeming It," Sermon Index, https://www.sermonindex.net/modules/articles/index.php?view=article&aid=3413, accessed October 28, 2022.

4   Edwards, "Time."

His point is that salvation happens in time. The opportunity every individual has for coming to Christ is restricted by the brevity of his or her life span. Everyone's eternal fate hinges on whether that person comes to Christ before his or her clock runs out. Therefore, time is exceedingly precious.

Second, time is precious because it is very short. We have all heard that basic principle of macroeconomics: supply and demand. The law of supply and demand says that the price of those resources which are more plentiful will drop, while the price of those which are scarcer will rise. But time is the scarcest resource of all and thus the most valuable.

James wrote of life's brevity, calling the whole sum of our time on this planet "a vapor" (James 4:14). Like the mist of your breath on a cold morning, your life will be here for a moment then it will suddenly be gone.

Similarly, Edwards wrote, "Time is so short, and the work which we have to do in it is so great, that we have none of it to spare. The work which we have to do to prepare for eternity, must be done in time, or it never can be done."[5]

If we are concerned about investing these lives well so that God is glorified and we receive the maximum reward as faithful stewards, hearing those words, "well done, good and faithful slave," then effective time management is of paramount importance for every Christian.

Third, time is precious because we do not know how much we have. We know our lives are brief, but we don't know how brief. It's easy to assume that we'll live to a ripe old age, but the truth is that none of us know how much longer we have. You could live to be a hundred years old or drop dead from a freak aneurism before you finish the next sentence.

We are not guaranteed a long life. As Edwards said, "We know not how little of it remains, whether a year, or several years, or only a month, a week, or a day. We are every day uncertain whether that day will not be the last, or whether we are to have the whole day."[6]

The clock is ticking and we don't know when the alarm will sound. This is a frightening truth for an unbeliever. But for a Christian who knows their eternity is secure in God's hand because of Jesus, the brevity of life simply becomes a motivator for good works.

Today is the day to serve the Lord with all my strength. Because I do not know if tomorrow will even come. Procrastination finds no home in the life of the man or woman who knows time may be up at any minute.

---

5   Edwards, "Time."

6   Edwards, "Time."

Fourth, time is precious because once gone, it's gone forever. Edwards wrote, "Time is very precious because when it is past, it cannot be recovered."[7]

We often hear talk of renewable vs. nonrenewable resources. Water, for example, is renewable because it can be recycled and used again, but oil, once it is burned up cannot be recovered to be used again.

But time is the ultimate nonrenewable resource. Once you use it, you cannot recover it, and you cannot drill for more of it. It's far more precious, therefore, than even money.

A person can lose his or her entire fortune, yet, given enough time, make it all back again. But when time is gone, it is truly gone. How often do we, in laziness, watch our days and hours circling the drain of worthless pursuits, as if what was being wasted was of no value? Too often we treat our time like the man using diamonds as kitty litter. We fail to esteem our minutes and days according to their true worth.

The expression, "our days are numbered" is based in Scripture. God has given us an allotted number of moments. Psalm 139:16 says, "In your book were all written, / The days that were ordained *for me,* / When as yet there was not one of them." But when one of those days is spent, it is spent forever.

Edwards emphasized this sobering reality by calling us to look back on the years wasted. "If we have lived fifty, or sixty, or seventy years, and have not improved our time, now it cannot be helped. It is eternally gone from us. All that we can do, is to improve the little that remains."[8]

Time is indeed precious.

You Have Enough Time

It can be easy to start to panic when you realize just how little time you have. I remember the first time I read that sermon; I was sitting outside of a coffee shop trying to hide my tears. I was on the cusp of turning thirty and I was overcome with guilt for how I'd wasted so much of my twenties.

However, the preciousness of time is not a message of despair, it is a message of hope. We can do nothing about what's gone before but to repent and ask the Lord's help in being better a steward of whatever time is left. He is a gracious God even toward time-squanderers like us.

There's another comfort to be found about time stewardship in the Scriptures as well: Though time is short, you have enough time.

---

7   Edwards, "Time."

8   Edwards, "Time."

Here it's necessary to counter-balance the reality of the brevity of our lives with a recognition that we know the One who holds the clock. God has indeed numbered our days. He is sovereign over our time. And that means God has given us exactly enough time to do what He has assigned us to do in this life.

We mentioned Ephesians 2:10 in Chapter 5, the verse that reads, "For we are His workmanship, created in Christ Jesus for good works, which God prepared beforehand, so that we would walk in them."

One thing that's easy to overlook in this verse is that the good works were "prepared beforehand" by God. This means God has specially prepared for you the good works He wants you to do in this life. And this should have profound implications for how we think about time stewardship.

Jesus in whom you "have obtained an inheritance, having been predestined according to His purpose who works all things after the counsel of His will," has also marked out for you the very stewardship you were designed for (Eph. 1:11). We can trust that the all-wise God has not given us an impossible task in those good works prepared for us. We can conclude that He has given us enough time to perform those good works. So, though time is short you have precisely enough of it to faithfully steward all that God has given you. So don't panic. Rejoice. Then get to work. Because there is no time to waste.

THREE COMMITMENTS FOR STEWARDING YOUR TIME WISELY

We could say many more things about time stewardship, and if you want more practical resources on this matter be sure to check out my ministry, Redeeming Productivity, which specializes in helping Christians learn how to steward their time more effectively.[9]

Next, let's look at three principals that can help guide our thinking on time stewardship, no matter what our lives look like.

First, be wary of wasting time. Perhaps the most obvious conclusion we should draw from seeing time as a stewardship is that we shouldn't waste it. In the parable of the talents the unfaithful steward buried his treasure in the ground. How often do we do that with the precious talent of time? How many hours do we bury in worthless pursuits? How much of the Lord's time do we invest into wicked forms of entertainment that only fill our minds

---

9　Visit redeemingproductivity.com for articles, podcasts, videos, and other resources on time stewardship. Or check out my book, *Redeeming Productivity: Getting More Done for the Glory of God* (Chicago: Moody Publishers, 2022).

with unrighteous thoughts? Rest and recreation are important parts of our stewardship too, but often what we call "sabbath" should really be called sloth. Time is a terrible thing to waste because it belongs to God.

Second, invest your time in quality over quantity of activities. Recognizing the shortness of time requires us to be focused. Charles Spurgeon said, "We must have only one aim. Had we plenty of time, we might try two or three schemes at once, though even then we should most probably fail for want of concentrating our energies; but as we have very little time, we had better economize it by attending to one thing. The man who devotes all his thought and strength to the accomplishment of one reasonable object is generally successful."[10]

It's easy for our time to be fragmented by the distractions constantly tugging at our attention. We must commit to work deeply with extreme focus on the good works God has uniquely called us to steward. If we don't, we will quickly be spread thin across many unrelated pursuits. Invest your time in a few high-quality activities that are most suited to your giftings.

Third, treat every day as an investment opportunity. Imagine if a friend told you that every day when he woke up an anonymous person had deposited $1,000 into his checking account with a memo that read, "Invest this however you see fit." But imagine that instead of investing the money, your friend was just withdrawing the money and spending on lavish meals and expensive clothes—and sometimes even misplacing piles of the money. "After all," he says, "I'll get another $1,000 tomorrow."

You'd be aghast, wouldn't you? But that's what we do with our time. Every morning we wake up with the gift of a new day to serve the master. Yet we greet these new mercies-filled days with the same attitude as the man with the $1,000, recklessly spending it on trivialities instead of investing for the long term. If you want to faithfully steward God's time, you must view each day as an investment opportunity. Where will you deposit the hours God has entrusted to you today?

ONE HABIT: KEEP A SCHEDULE

Now that we've talked about the principles of time stewardship, let me leave you with a simple habit. I am constantly surprised at how many Christian adults simply do not know how to practically manage their time. But unless someone has taught you how to manage your time, how would you know? The simplest place to start in being a better time steward is to begin with

10   Charles Spurgeon, "The Time is Short," *Metropolitan Tabernacle Pulpit* Vol. 49.

keeping a schedule. Many people recognize the wisdom of keeping a budget for their finances. They know money is an important resource that shouldn't be squandered. But few are as diligent with how they spend their time. Keeping a schedule simply means having a budget for your time.

When I say keep a schedule, I don't just mean putting appointments on your calendar (though you should certainly do this). I mean having a plan for how you spend your days and weeks. Too many believers live their work lives in reactive mode. They go to their job, do the next thing on the list, respond to the next crises, then go home. There's no strategy, no plan.

The same is true of many homemakers as well. They rush to clean the house only when guests are coming over or only run to the grocery store before every meal. They aren't planning.

The same is true of many Christian students as well. Instead of budgeting their time, they scramble to get assignments done right before the deadline or cram for the test the night before. Living in reactive mode is exhausting. It's also poor stewardship.

Sometimes we do have to exist in reactive mode for a season, but we should never make a habit of living there. It's easy to slip into this mode where emergencies write our schedules for us, isn't it? But if we take seriously our call to time stewardship, then we must take seriously the responsibility of writing our own schedule.

You alone are accountable for how you steward the time God has entrusted to you. This is the difference between being proactive and reactive. Proactive Christians have a plan; they have a schedule. Being proactive is the only way we can ensure that we are investing our time into the things that matter most to God and not just being ruled by the tyranny of the urgent.

Keeping a schedule does not need to be complicated. A simple way to start keeping a schedule is to take a little time at the start of the new week to look at the days ahead and decide what you will work on. What are the big tasks that need doing? How will you push that project ahead? And most importantly, how will you invest this week for the Master?

Then, do the same thing each morning. Before you start the day in earnest, make a plan. I like to write out the hours of the day down the left side of a piece of paper, then block out what I intend to do during each hour. I don't always stick to the schedule perfectly, but I know that by writing it out I will be investing my time more intentionally that day.

Time is the most precious resource of all. So as good stewards for Christ, let's make sure that we are investing it intentionally for Him every single day.

Study Questions

1. Why is time such a precious resource?

2. What are some of the things that most tempt you to waste time?

3. Do you ever get anxious about time? How are you comforted to know that God has given enough time to do what He's called us to do?

4. How does thinking about time in financial terms (e.g. in terms of investment, budgeting, etc.) help us better steward it?

5. Do you keep a schedule? What are some practical ways you can improve your time stewardship?

7

STEWARDING YOUR TALENT

As each one has received a special *gift, employ it in serving one another as good stewards of the manifold grace of God.*

First Peter 4:10

A T THE BEGINNING OF this book, I noted that the way Jesus used the word "talents" in the parable of the talents was not the same way we use that term today. He was talking about a unit of money, whereas we use talent to refer to skills or abilities. But there is a historical reason why we call our skills and abilities talents. And they are indeed things that need to be invested carefully as part of a plan for total life stewardship.

Somewhere around the mid-fifteenth century, the word talent came to be associated with a special natural ability, a unique aptitude, or a gift a person had been loaned for use and improvement.[1] And this association is apt. Because if all of life is a stewardship, then so are our natural gifts and abilities. And faithful stewardship includes strategically deploying your unique abilities for God.

Stewardship of all our gifts, natural and spiritual, is the vocation of every believer. And a wonderful by-product of faithfully stewarding your talents is that it also leads to personal fulfillment. What could be more satisfying than performing the role God has custom designed for you?

YOUR NATURAL TALENTS

For the purposes of this chapter, when we talk about talents in the sense of skill or ability, we will include not just natural giftedness but also trained skill. A talented basketball player does not just happen to be tall and possess innate athletic ability but has trained for years to shoot a consistent free throw and master the fundamentals of the game. We can think of our

---

1   "Talent | Etymology, Origin and Meaning of Talent by Etymonline," Etymonline, https://www.etymonline.com/word/talent (accessed Oct. 12, 2022).

natural talents in two categories: physical talents and mental talents. Both require careful stewardship.

Stewarding Your Body

Physical talents include abilities that have to do with the body. Think physical strength, dexterity, skill in craftsmanship (Exod. 35:10), or even musical skill (Ps. 33:3–4). As our culture has moved from being centered less on physical labor and more on mental labor, it's easy for us to neglect the stewardship of our physical bodies. But your physical abilities are part of your stewardship before God.

I've had friends in the trades who have confessed to feeling less than intelligent because, instead of working at a computer earning a living with their minds, they are skilled with their hands and physical bodies. But your unique giftings are given to you by the God who custom designed you for a definite purpose.

> For You formed my inward parts;
> You wove me in my mother's womb.
> I will give thanks to You, for I am fearfully and wonderfully made;
> Wonderful are your works,
> And my soul knows it very well.
> My frame was not hidden from You,
> When I was being made in secret,
> *And* skillfully wrought in the depths of the earth.
> Your eyes have seen my unformed substance;
> And in Your book were all written,
> The days that were ordained *for* me,
> When as yet there was not one of them.   (Ps. 139:13–16)

Those with physical prowess have the joyous privilege of being able to build things in the physical world. They can protect others from danger and serve through the ministry of physical presence. So often our preference for mental talent leaves us with Christians who serve in word but neglect to serve in deed (1 John 3:18). Your physical body and the things you can do with it are part of your stewardship.

We should also consider that even our physical shortcomings can be talents to be stewarded. Our God delights to use the weak to shame the strong (1 Cor. 1:26–27).

Many believers have found their physical weaknesses to be an occasion for being mightily used by God. I think of believers like Joni Eareckson

Tada or Justin Peters, who are unable to walk. These two would both tell you that though they require the use of wheelchairs, God has used them not despite but *through* their disabilities.

Many who are unable to speak have crashed the gates of heaven with ceaseless prayer. Others unable to see have honored God with their eyes of faith. And many who are unable to put one foot in front of the other have walked by faith in daily obedience. I think in heaven we will be pleasantly surprised to see how many crowns array the heads of those who went through this life with broken bodies.

STEWARDING YOUR MIND

A second category of natural talent is our mental abilities. God has gifted many believers with incredibly sharp minds. However, there is always the temptation to boast about our intellect or to use it merely to serve ourselves. But life stewards see the mind as just one more talent to invest for the Master. The Bible calls us to both guard and grow our minds.

One way we steward our minds is by guarding them. The Scriptures encourage us to guard our hearts and minds (Phil. 4:6–7), to take thoughts captive to obey Christ (2 Cor. 10:5), and to be watchful when it comes to our minds (1 Pet. 1:13; 4:7). Guarding your mind means being careful about what you put into it. If you fill your head with entertainment that glorifies sin, or promotes worldviews that are contrary to Scripture, you're simply inviting temptation into your life.

Positively, guarding your mind means filling it with truth. We must fill our heads with the Word of God and hear it echoed to us in our local church and by other faithful believers. We need constant reminders that cut through the world's noise with the clarity of God's truths.

We also steward our minds not just by guarding them but also by growing them. Be diligent about having your mind not conformed to the world's ways of thinking but renewed by exposure to God's truth (Rom. 12:2). Growing your mind also means training your mind not just in spiritual things, but for use in all of life. Just as Paul disciplined his body (1 Cor. 9:27), we must discipline our minds. Read good books, solve difficult problems, push yourself to grow in your thinking and reasoning so your mind will be a sharp weapon in God's arsenal.

And most importantly, as we guard and grow our minds, we need to invest them in worthy pursuits. Give the best of your mental abilities to serve your local church, your neighbors, and your family. God has entrusted you with your mind. Your role as a steward is to make a good return on that trust.

One thing we must avoid when it comes to our natural talents, however, is the danger of trusting in or boasting in our abilities. "Some *boast* in chariots and some in horses, but we will boast in the name of the LORD our God" (Ps. 20:7). We must remember that these are not things we have created but are gifts of God (1 Cor. 4:7). An arrogant steward is an abomination. "GOD IS OPPOSED THE PROUD BUT GIVES GRACE TO THE HUMBLE" (James 4:6). So as you use your natural talents, make sure you always do so with an attitude of humility. The whole point of stewardship is to use these gifts to make God look good, not yourself.

Besides natural talents, another stewardship must be discharged in faithfulness as well—that is our spiritual talents.

YOUR SPIRITUAL TALENTS

You will recall that the occasion for Jesus' parables in Matthew 25 was the Olivet Discourse. Jesus was preparing the disciples for His departure and entrusting them with the advancement of His kingdom. The disciples were being handed a baton, and it was just about time for them to run the next leg of this spiritual race.

God certainly uses our physical and mental talents, but the kingdom of God advances supernaturally. It is a spiritual kingdom that moves forward one heart at a time. And it grows through the faithful proclamation of the gospel and the ministry of the body of believers one to another. That is why stewarding our spiritual talents is so important.

We will talk about two spiritual talents here: the gospel and your spiritual gifts. The gospel is for bringing in new citizens of God's kingdom, and your spiritual gifts are for building them up.

The gospel itself is a stewardship. Several years ago, I was teaching a course on stewardship, and a student came to me with a concern. He thought it was a stretch to say the talents in the parable represented money, natural talents, time, or even spiritual gifts. He said his pastor had told him the talents represented the gospel and nothing else. But that interpretation doesn't make sense if you apply it consistently to the passage. For example, you end up having to say awkward things like that the reward for faithfulness in the gospel is more gospel, or that Christ takes the gospel away from unfaithful stewards and gives it those who already have the gospel (Matt. 25:21, 23, 28). As I've said in this book, I believe Jesus had something more holistic in mind when He used this parable to encourage His disciples to be faithful servants.

Nevertheless, I do believe the gospel is part of every Christian's stewardship. However, it's not the only part of our stewardship. And the gospel is the particular stewardship of those called to full-time ministry. Paul spoke of being "entrusted with the gospel" (1 Thess. 2:4; 1 Tim. 1:11), and called apostles and evangelists "stewards of the mysteries of God" (1 Cor. 4:1). But how does one steward the gospel?

We steward the gospel of Jesus Christ in several ways. First, we steward the gospel by believing it. When someone shares the good news with you, the proper response is to believe it and receive it with joy.

Second, we steward the gospel by living faithfully. True believers will bear the fruit of saving faith (James 2:24–26).

Third, we steward the gospel by sharing it. Not everyone is called to full-time ministry, and not all are evangelists, but all are called to share the good news of the gospel.

I've often heard ministers compare keeping the gospel to yourself as akin to a person living in a cancer ward at a hospital who has the cure for cancer but refuses to tell the other patients. Faithful Christians proclaim the gospel to their neighbors because they want to see their neighbors saved and because faithful stewards long to see their King's kingdom expand. This expansion comes by hearing and believing the gospel. And hearing the gospel requires that someone preach it (Rom. 10:17).

The other half of our spiritual stewardship is our spiritual gifts. The Scriptures teach that every believer has been gifted by God through the Holy Spirit. And these spiritual gifts are a stewardship to be used to serve the church. "As each one has received a *special* gift, employ it in serving one another as good stewards of the manifold grace of God" (1 Pet. 4:10).

The New Testament has at least seven lists of spiritual gifts that God gives to believers.[2] Some of these lists are about gifts for certain offices, such as apostles, prophets, and teachers (Eph. 4:11). But others speak more generally about gifts distributed to every believer (Rom. 12:6–8; 1 Pet. 4:10–11; 1 Cor. 12). These are spiritual talents, and they are different from our natural talents.

It's amazing to consider that God Himself has hand-picked a special gift for you to enable you to serve His church. Just like the stewards in

---

2   John MacArthur, Richard Mayhue. *Biblical Doctrine: A Systematic Summary of Bible Truth* (Wheaton, IL: Crossway, 2017), 379.

the parable, the Master has carefully selected what He would like you to oversee. "But one and the same Spirit works all these things, distributing to each one individually just as He wills" (1 Cor. 12:11). These special gifts in areas such as teaching, exhorting, giving, leading, mercy, speaking, serving, wisdom, knowledge, faith, discernment, and helping, are spiritual talents. And they are to be stewarded faithfully.

Too many believers treat church as if it's a spectator sport. If you're not preaching or singing, you can feel as if your role is just to watch. But this is not true. The body of Christ is all about participation. No one should be standing on the sidelines.

To put a sharper point on it, if you are involved in a church but not using your spiritual gifts for the common good, you are acting like the wicked servant who buried the master's treasure instead of investing it. If you take nothing else away from this book, as your first step to more faithful stewardship you should determine to find a place to serve your local church this week. Faithfulness requires it.

Three Commitments for Stewarding Your Talents

As our natural and spiritual talents vary from person to person, I want to leave you with three principles that will apply no matter what your giftings are. These three commitments will ensure that you are faithfully stewarding the talents the Lord has entrusted to you.

First, seek God's glory not yours. It is very easy for those with prodigious skills—whether natural or spiritual—to look at their abilities as a way to make themselves look good. But to understand how horrendous this attitude is, consider what this might have looked like in the parable of the talents. Imagine if after the master departed, one of the stewards who had been entrusted with more talents had turned around and rubbed it in the faces of his fellow servants. "Look at that. The master entrusted me with five talents and you guys only have two and one! Guess we know who the better steward is." Then imagine if in his arrogance he had taken the master's money and decided to spend it on himself with the aim of impressing his fellow servants with how great he was.

We'd say that servant was a pompous fool, wouldn't we? After all it wasn't even his money. In reality, he had nothing to boast in. And in spending the master's money for his own glory, he was storing up wrath for himself for when the master returned from his journey. In the same way, if you use your physical or spiritual talents for your own glory, you are stealing from God and dishonoring your fellow stewards. That's the opposite of faithfulness.

Second, serve others with your talents. First Corinthians 12:7 says the purpose of spiritual gifts was the edification of other believers: "But to each one is given the manifestation of the Spirit for the common good."

Paul spent a great deal of time rebuking the Corinthians who used their spiritual gifts as a pedestal to elevate their own egos while making other believers feel inferior. All your gifts are opportunities for service. That includes your natural as well as your spiritual gifts.

Just look at Jesus, the most gifted man to ever live, He said that He "did not come to be served, but to serve, and to give His life a ransom for many" (Matt. 20:28). Faithful stewardship in Christ's church is a mission of service and sacrifice, not self-aggrandizement.

Our talents equip us for that mission. Our talents are our ticket to pursue greatness with our lives—but not in the way we often think. Jesus said that true greatness does not come through self-promotion, bragging, or pursuing the praise of the world. Instead, greatness comes through humility. Greatness comes through service. "The greatest among you shall be your servant" (23:11).

As long as we have these sinful bodies, we will feel the awful desire to have others call us master instead of servant. But we must always remember we are stewards, and stewards are required to be found faithful.

Third, improve your talents. Don't let your skills, abilities, and gifts atrophy. Has someone ever complimented you on a skill or feature you didn't even realize you had? I remember being at a fast-food restaurant one time with my wife when the girl taking our order started going on and on about how much she envied my wife's eye lashes. Afterward my wife said to me, "No one has ever complimented me on my eyelashes." She had no idea.

In the same way we are often the worst judges of our own gifts. Sometimes we are oblivious to them. But once people make us aware of them, it's our job to put them to good use.

Especially when it comes to our spiritual gifts, we can be tempted by a grass-is-always-greener syndrome. We spend our time peeking over the fence at the amazing teaching ability of this neighbor or the mental acumen of that neighbor. But while we are envying them, our own lawns are dying for lack of water. As the parable implies, talents are meant to be improved, and this is true of our natural and spiritual talents as well. You must use your talents to improve your talents.

A person who has a spiritual gift of teaching must work to hone that gift. He should be a better teacher a year from now than he is today. Paul warned Timothy, "Do not neglect the spiritual gift within you, which was bestowed on you through prophetic utterance with the laying on of hands by the presbytery. Take pains with these things; be *absorbed* in them, so that your progress will be evident to all" (1 Tim. 4:14–15). This young pastor was not to let his gift wither but was to demonstrate observable progress.

The same is true of any gift. If you are a talented musician, part of stewardship is advancing that talent through practice. If you are talented in administration, study to lead better and improve your organization.

At the end of the day, we must remember that our talents are not our treasure to bury. The failure of the steward who buried his one talent in the ground was not that he lost the talent, but that he didn't put it to use. He did not lose it, but he also didn't improve it. Are you improving your talents, or have you tucked them away in the attic to rot?

All of these commitments require the diligence that marks a faithful steward. They require a zeal that keeps us going day after day (Rom. 12:11). And they require a commitment to working hard. "Whatever you do, do your work heartily, as for the Lord rather than for men, knowing that from the Lord you will receive the reward of the inheritance. It is the Lord Christ whom you serve" (Col. 3:23–24). But in the end, the hard work of faithful stewardship will be worth it because God rewards faithfulness.

ONE HABIT: SEEK OPPORTUNITIES

One habit that will help you to always make the most of your natural and spiritual talents is to cultivate the discipline of seeking commitments that suit your abilities. If you're going to steward a talent, solicit opportunities to use it.

This means, if possible, you should pursue a vocation that uses your gifts. Too many Christians settle for jobs that pay the bills while squandering their talents. If you have the opportunity to find a job that provides for you and your family while using your unique giftings, you owe it to God and to yourself to take advantage of that opportunity.

Seeking out opportunities to use your talents also means making your church aware of your spiritual giftings. Don't be arrogant, demanding a place to serve. But humbly say, "I believe I'm gifted in this; I'd love to serve the church in some way with my giftings."

There are no sweeter words to a pastor's ears than "I'd like to serve." And this is how you steward your spiritual gifts to build up the church.

When you are on the lookout for ways to use your gifts, you'll find them. Remember, God wants us to be faithful stewards, having prepared in advance the good works we are to walk in (Eph. 2:10). That should give you confidence that the opportunities to use your gifts are out there. But you need to always be on the lookout for them. That's just what faithful stewards do; they use their talents.

Study Questions:

1. What's a unique natural talent you have?

2. Why do you think it's important that we find ways to use and improve our skills and abilities?

3. How do spiritual talents differ from natural ones?

4. Do you know your spiritual gifts? What are they?

5. Do you feel you are using the full scope of your talents right now? What could you do to find ways to use them more effectively?

8

STEWARDING YOUR TREASURE

Each one must do *just as he has purposed in his heart, not grudgingly*
or under compulsion, for God loves a cheerful giver.

Second Corinthians 9:7

SOMETHING ABOUT the topic of financial stewardship makes Christians feel very uncomfortable. I still remember the Sunday I visited the
church of my parents' friends when I was a kid. It was a "Tithing emphasis
Sunday." The church had called in a specialist to preach to the congregation
about giving.

When the adults finally realized what was happening, it was like the air
was sucked out of the room. Even as a kid I noticed how the adults stiffened
up and clutched their wallets and purses. I don't remember much about
the sermon, but I remember the nervous joking afterwards as the adults
discussed the sermon in the lobby and parking lot.

Discussions about money and tithing can be awkward. When the pastor
starts talking about giving, you may suddenly feel like you're stuck in one of
those high-pressure time-share sales seminars, wondering how you got suck-
ered into this for a free meal voucher. You might feel this way for various
reasons, including having been part of churches that served up their financial requests with two heaping scoops of guilt and social pressure. Whatever
your experience regarding this topic, financial stewardship is indeed a critical component of life stewardship. We cannot ignore this topic.

As we reach the financial component of stewardship, the message is no
different from all the other areas of life stewardship we've discussed already.
Just as with your time and talents, your money and possessions are on loan
to you from God. Your job as a steward is to use those resources in a way
that most glorifies Him.

When it comes to financial stewardship, however, many of us have heard
so many conflicting messages that it can be quite confusing. Maybe you feel

paralyzed as to what exactly financial stewardship entails. Perhaps you've asked questions like these:

- Is tithing for today?
- Is it wrong to be rich?
- How much is too much?
- Isn't money the root of all evil?
- Is it wrong to spend money on fun things?
- How much should I be giving to my church?

In this chapter, we will look at several biblical principles regarding financial stewardship, identify three commitments for having a right attitude toward money, and present one practical habit that will help you steward this important resource well.

WHY MONEY MATTERS TO GOD

Have you ever considered why the way you use your money matters to God? When it comes to giving to the local church, for example, does God really need our money? I mean, He's in control of everything, isn't He? God owns it all (Ps. 24:1). He owns the cattle on a thousand hills, He doesn't need our measly 10 percent (50:10). "If I were hungry, I would not tell you, For the world is Mine, and all it contains" (50:12).

We're talking about the God who created the entire universe using just His words (33:6). This is the Jesus who multiplied fishes and loaves to feed a crowd of five thousand (Mark 6:30–44). God doesn't need our money. But He does care how we use it. And He does ask us to use it to give. In fact, more than a quarter of Jesus' parables deal directly with financial matters.[1]

Money matters to God because how we use our money is an expression of our values. How we use our money shows where our hope lies. To put it simply, how you steward your money and possessions shows exactly what your faith is really in. As Randy Alcorn said, "Our use of money and possessions is a decisive statement of our eternal values. What we do with our money loudly affirms which kingdom we belong to."[2]

Our attitude toward money is directly related to our spiritual condition. Look at Zacchaeus for example. His spiritual transformation was immediately accompanied by a transformation in his relationship to money. He went

---

1   Randy Alcorn, *Money, Possessions, and Eternity* (Carol Stream, IL: Tyndale, 1989), 141.

2   Randy Alcorn, *Money, Possessions, and Eternity*, xv.

from swindling others to returning four times what he stole (Luke 19:1–10)! Or consider the rich young ruler who asked Jesus how he might inherit eternal life, and Jesus' probing revealed that the man's real god was his money (Mark 10:17–27). God tells us how to steward our money, not because He needs it, but because He wants us to become certain kind of people.

When John the Baptist came preaching repentance, the people asked him about spiritual realities, and his answers nearly always concerned monetary matters. He told them to share their clothes and food with the poor as the fruits of repentance. He told tax collectors to stop stealing. He told soldiers to stop extorting money but to be content with their wages (Luke 3:7–14).

These people weren't asking about money, they were asking about spiritual transformation. But "John couldn't talk about spirituality without talking in terms of how we handle our money and possessions."[3]

How a person views money is one of the most accurate gauges of their spiritual condition. Richard C. Halverson, who served as Chaplain of the United States Senate in the 1980s and 1990s, summed it up nicely when he said:

> Jesus Christ said more about money than about any other single thing because, when it comes to a man's real nature, money is of first importance. Money is an exact index to a man's true character. All through Scripture there is an intimate correlation between the development of a man's character and how he handles his money.[4]

God cares about how we use our money, not because He needs it but because how we use our money is an expression of where our heart is. And the truth is money comes preloaded with a host of temptations that can keep us from walking closely with God and fulfilling our role as stewards.

Lies Money Tells

One of the most frequently misquoted verses in the Bible is First Timothy 6:10. How often have you heard someone say that money is the root of all evil? That's not what the verse says. It actually says, "For the love of money is a *root* of all sorts of evils." The problem isn't money, but our attitude toward money, because money can be incredibly deceptive.[5]

---

3   Randy Alcorn, *Money, Possessions and Eternity*, 5–6

4   Randy Alcorn, *Money, Possessions and Eternity*, 3.

5   Adapted from an article originally published in The Master's Seminary Blog. Reagan Rose, "The Deceitfulness of Riches: 3 Lies Money Tells," https://blog.tms.edu/3-lies-money-tells, (accessed Oct. 17, 2022).

In the parable of the sower, Jesus taught a crowd of followers about the various reasons people reject the message of the Kingdom (Matt. 13:1–9). In the parable, the message of the Kingdom was referred to as a seed, and those who heard it were compared to four different types of soils: a path, rocky soil, thorny soil, and good soil. The parable is unique from other parables because after telling it, Jesus gave an extended private explanation of its meaning to His disciples (13:18–23). We aren't left to speculate what it means; Jesus explained it.

The seed that falls along the path is what happens "When anyone hears word of the kingdom and does not understand it, the evil *one* comes and snatches away what has been sown in his heart" (13:19). The rocky soil is the one "who hears the word and immediately receives it with joy, yet he has no *firm* root in himself," so when trouble comes, he falls away (13:20–21). Then there's the thorny soil, "this is the man who hears the word, and the worry of the world and the deceitfulness of wealth choke the word, and it becomes unfruitful" (13:22). Finally, there is the good soil, the person who hears the word, understands it, and bears much fruit (13:23).

I want to focus your attention on one statement concerning the thorny soil. Our Lord says that the word is choked out in this person because of the cares of the world and "the deceitfulness of wealth."

That phrase has always intrigued me. Money is just a thing; how could it be deceitful? People say, "Money talks" but Jesus said, "Money lies." So, what kind of lies does money tell us? There are at least three big lies people believe about money. And if we aren't careful, even Christians can fall prey to these fiscal falsehoods.

Lie #1: Money Is the Goal of Life

The first lie money tells is that money is the goal of life. This one seems so obvious on the surface that we might assume it is easily avoided. But the world screams this philosophy in our faces daily. Every commercial, every celebrity, every new car our neighbor purchases, dangles that carrot called "success" before our eyes.

If we don't watch carefully, before we know it, we may find our days consumed with doing whatever it takes to get that next raise, comparing ourselves to others, and constantly asking, "Have I made it yet?" But chasing money as the goal of life is a race that no one wins.

Here's a simple test: When deciding whether something would be good for you or your family to do, is your first question, "How will this honor

God?" or "Will this be good for our family?" Or is it, like for so many of us, "How much will this cost?"

Financial responsibility is important, but when money becomes the primary decision-making criteria for everything we do, that may indicate that we have started to believe the lie that money is the ultimate goal.

The antidote to this potent lie is the truth that the Christian's ultimate life goal can never be something as temporary as money. Our Lord had a simple rhetorical question that upends this philosophy of financial success. He said, "For what will it profit a man if he gains the whole world and forfeits his soul?" (Matt. 16:26).

Money is not the goal of life. Setting our focus on acquiring earthly riches is pathetically shortsighted in light of eternity. We aren't to be anxious about money or the things it provides. Instead, our Lord said, "But seek first His kingdom and His righteousness, and all these things will be added to you" (6:33).

Lie #2: Money Will Keep Me Safe

The second lie money tells is that riches hold the key to security. A recent movement among the millennial generation advocates for individual "financial independence." This crowd focuses on developing passive income strategies and "wealth hacks." In many cases, they suggest practicing extreme frugality so you can save up enough to retire in your thirties or forties. Then you can spend your days traveling the world or simply living out your life without financial worry.

Many of the books and blogs advocating financial independence talk about something called the "4 percent rule." The idea is that if you can save up and invest twenty-five times your yearly expenses, then you no longer have to work because you can live off the interest by withdrawing just 4 percent a year from your investments while not touching the principal.

With the right amount of hustle, that's something a young person can achieve—and indeed many have achieved. That's the dream, right? No boss, no 9-to-5, just pure freedom. That is the allure of financial independence.

I can see some of you opening Excel right now to run the calculations for how you, too, can become financially independent and retire early. But let me ask you a few questions first. Is anything wrong with being financially independent? No, of course not. But how about this question: Why does it sound so enticing? Sure, it's the freedom to do what you want and go where you want, but I think the promise of safety is what's so alluring.

If you were financially independent, you would no longer have to live paycheck to paycheck. You wouldn't have to worry about money. You would be secure. At least that's the promise of this lie money tells us.

The perniciousness of this lie money tells is evidenced in the apparent nobility of the idea of financial independence. From the outside this pursuit looks like it is avoiding the avarice of the first lie. It's not viewing money as the goal of life at all.

Gurus of this lifestyle advocate for honorable-sounding principles like simple living, frugality, and a focus on experiences and relationships over collecting possessions. That makes it hard to condemn them as being materialistic or greedy. But behind this pursuit of financial independence is the lie that money will provide us with security.

The truth is that riches bring no genuine security. You can lose it all in a moment. Money cannot be trusted to protect us. Solomon wrote, "He who trusts in his riches will fall, / But the righteous will flourish like the *green leaf*" (Prov. 11:28). Trusting in riches is actually a form of idolatry. Whether we trust in money for happiness or security, we are putting it in the place of God. But money is a poor object for our faith. Christ alone is adequate as a trustworthy source of security. Through financial highs and economic downturns, no matter if you're rich or poor, Christ is the one you should trust for your sense of security.

Look what the writer to the Hebrews says, "*Make sure that* your character is free from the love of money, being content with what you have; for He Himself has said, 'I will never desert you, nor will I ever forsake you,' so that we confidently say, 'The Lord is my helper, I will not be afraid. / What will man do to me?'" (Heb. 13:5–6). Now that's true security!

Lie #3: Money Is an Easy Master

The third lie money tells is that it is an easy master. Though we might look to money to provide freedom, money wants to enslave us. It seems more comfortable in many respects to serve cash rather than Christ. No cumbersome rules, no self-sacrifice, and definitely no pesky tithes making a dent in my budget! But money is a hard master.

While a Christian would not openly admit to serving money as his or her master, many believers try to split the difference. Secretly we think, "I'll serve Christ some, and I'll serve money a little," or "Jesus can have the 10 percent, but the rest is mine." But the Scriptures are clear—you can't have it both ways. Jesus Christ has a no-moonlighting policy. "You cannot serve God and wealth" (Matt. 6:24).

What's more, money is not the easier master. The dollar is fickle. Money will raise your hopes on the upward slope of the stock market, then shove them off the cliff of the next market dip. The dollar will promise you happiness if you sacrifice your family and friends to gain a little more. But if you serve it, in the end money will leave you alone, broken, and eternally bereft.

Worst of all even if you find financial success and buy everything you dreamed of owning, the dollar refuses to fulfill its promise of a life of ease and comfort. As the adage goes, before you know it, the things you own begin to own you.

Many who have found financial success have discovered that instead of giving freedom, money delivered shackles. Every possession, every investment, every business requires more of your attention to hold it all together. Soon, what felt like freedom begins to feel like slavery. What promised peace of mind brings more headaches and worry. Money is a hard master, and it will leave you exhausted if you choose to be its slave.

The truth is Christ is the easier Master. Jesus said, "For My yoke is easy and My burden is light" (11:30). Following the Lord is not without its pains. However, in the long run, putting your trust in the One who has already paid it all is the wisest path and leads to the longest-lasting riches.

WHAT ABOUT TITHING?

Much ink has been spilled throughout church history concerning the place of the tithe for New Covenant believers. I'm sure this chapter won't be the final word that puts the debates to rest. But a few principles are worth noting regarding the practice of giving 10 percent of your income to the church. For further reading on this subject and general financial stewardship, I recommend Randy Alcorn's *Money, Possessions and Eternity*. This is the best work I know of on how money fits into a Christian worldview. But let me leave you with three principles about the tithe that should help as you think about how giving fits into your financial stewardship.

Tithing Is Not a New Testament Concept

First, the tithe is not a New Testament concept. When someone brings up the tithe, we think it means giving 10 percent of your income to the church. But this idea is not found in the New Testament. It has its roots in an Old Testament practice performed by the nation of Israel under the Mosaic law.

Those who import this practice wholesale into how Christians should give to the church do so without warrant. Let's look at the Old Testament tithe to understand why it is not so easily transferred to a New Covenant context.

As we examine the tithe, keep in mind that being part of an agrarian society, the Israelite's tithes were not in the form of money or coinage. They didn't use money until the late sixth century when the Persians minted coins. Instead, for most Old Testament saints, "a tithe was a tenth part of the grain or olive harvest, a tenth part of the grape crop, and a tenth part of the animals one raised."[6] But matters are further complicated when you realize the Old Testament teachings had three different types of tithes.

First, there was a tithe that went to the temple in Jerusalem, where whole families ate their own tithes in and around the temple grounds. This was more akin to a Thanksgiving dinner than dropping an envelope in the offering plate. It was done to recognize that harvesting crops and raising animals was a result of God's blessing (Deut. 14:22–33).

Second, every three years, a tithe was stored in a person's hometown and became a sort of reserve that the Levites could draw on, since they did not receive a portion of the Promised Land like the other tribes (Josh. 13:33). This tithe was shared with widows, orphans, and resident aliens. And many of the promises of blessings we read about that accompany generosity in giving specifically relate to this tithe (Deut. 14:28–29). We might think of this more like the "benevolent offerings" many churches do to support those in need within the congregation or surrounding community.

Third was a tithe to support the Levitical priests even more directly. This type of tithe is the closest to what we typically mean when we talk about a tithe in a New Covenant context.

The Levites were the pastors of Israel. This gift was given to support their ministry. We read in Numbers 18:20–32 that this tithe was called an "offering to Yahweh." It compensated the Levites who did not have any income from owning or working the land.

Failure to fulfill this obligation was accompanied by the death penalty (just see what happens if you implement that in your church's tithing program). To not give this tithe was compared to stealing from God. But giving it would result in blessing (Mal. 3:6–11).[7]

---

6   Ralph W. Klein, "Stewardship in the Old Testament." *Currents in Theology and Mission* 36, no. 5 (October 2009): 332.

7   Klein, 330–334.

We might summarize the purpose of the various Old Testament tithes as: (1) An opportunity to rejoice in God's provision and express thanks for it, (2) a means to provide adequate food for the needy, and (3) a means to support the clergy and their ministry. Notably, not all these tithes were obligatory, and not all of them concerned giving to the religious class.

So, though the third type of tithe is similar to what we practice in our churches today, there does not appear to be a similar command for New Testament believers that makes giving 10 percent to the church obligatory.

Giving and generosity are important for Christians, but are never presented as mandatory in the same way they were in Old Testament Israel.

Ten Percent Is Not the Standard

Second, 10 percent is not the standard. You will not find this number anywhere in the New Testament in relation to giving.

Perhaps, as some preachers have said, 10 percent might make a worthy goal to aim for. But in some cases, it may be more than a person can afford, and for others, it may be far too little. Let's not forget the widow in the temple who gave just two copper coins, but it was all she had (Mark 12:41–44).

You certainly should give to your church. Paul actually went out of his way to say that elders and pastors who "rule well" should "be considered worthy of double honor, especially those who work hard at preaching and teaching" (1 Tim. 5:17). It is right to support your pastors financially because "the laborer is worthy of his wages" (5:18). In fact, the Bible says ministers have a right to receive financial remuneration for their spiritual services. "If we sowed spiritual things in you, is it too much if we reap material things from you?" (1 Cor. 9:11). But the New Testament simply does not tell us how much we are to give to the church.

Giving that pleases God is a matter of the heart. Matters of the heart are not easily quantified. In fact, while 10 percent might sound like a great goal, it can lead us to some bad conclusions about financial stewardship.

The truth is not that 10 percent of your money belongs to God—all of it does. It's easy for us to think that if we give 10 percent to the church, then our financial stewardship has been fulfilled. However, "It is a serious mistake to assume that if an individual gives ten per cent of his income to his church he is a good steward. His stewardship depends just as much on what he does with the remaining ninety per cent as on the ten per cent."[8]

---

8   George D. Kelsey, "An Interpretation of the Doctrine of Stewardship." *Review & Expositor,* 50, no. 2 (April 1953): 190.

Giving Is an Act of Faith

Third, giving must be an act of faith, not presumption. Scripture presents the promise of temporal reward for financial giving (Prov. 3:9–10; 19:17; Mal. 3:6–11; Luke 6:38; 2 Cor. 9:6).

The Bible often says those who give not only receive spiritual rewards, but also financial ones. Some people, however, have taken this principle and reduced it to a law that preys on people's greed. The so-called "prosperity gospel" is a type of preaching that promises financial blessings for those who sow a seed of faith (a financial gift).[9]

This mentality turns stewardship on its head. Instead of it being a faith-filled exercise in gratitude, giving becomes an act of presumption akin to throwing a coin in a fountain so you can get your wish. The offering plate becomes a magic box—give it a dollar, and it will turn it into ten. The prosperity gospel transforms giving from an act of worshiping God into an act of idolizing Mammon.

It is true that temporal blessing often accompanies Christian generosity. And we should not ignore this very biblical principle merely because some false teachers have abused this teaching. But making the hope of financial reward into the motivation for giving seriously perverts Christian generosity. As Tilley notes:

> It is one thing, however, to make descriptive statements concerning what often accompanies the faithful exercise of stewardship and quite another to parade these as the exclusive or even primary motivation for faithful stewardship.[10]

That type of giving is an act of presumption. Instead, giving is to be an act of faith. When we give, we are saying, "All of this belongs to you anyway, God." And we are trusting that the same God who enabled us to earn that money that we are giving will continue to provide for us in all things. When we give, we are trusting that the God who clothes the lilies and feeds the sparrows will provide for our needs even as we return to Him a portion of what He has entrusted to us (Matt. 6:26–34).

---

9   For an excellent treatment on the errors and dangers of the prosperity gospel read Costi W. Hinn, *God, Greed, and the (Prosperity) Gospel: How Truth Overwhelms a Life Built on Lies* (Grand Rapids: Zondervan, 2019).

10 W. Clyde Tilley, "A Biblical Approach to Stewardship." *Review & Expositor* 84 (3): 439.

THREE COMMITMENTS

Considering all these things, let's look at three commitments that must mark our financial stewardship—not just as it concerns giving money to the church, but also in how we manage money and possessions in all of life.

First, be a cheerful giver. Second Corinthians 9:7 gives very succinct instruction about giving and the Christian: "Each one *must do* just as he has purposed in his heart, not grudgingly or under compulsion, for God loves a cheerful giver."

Giving is not a matter of percentages, but of the heart. It's not a matter of being guilted into giving but doing it out of an abundant joy. Heavy-handed appeals for Christian giving rob believers of the joy and promises of giving from the heart. It is, after all, "more blessed to give than to receive" (Acts 20:35). So, as you give make sure that you are giving from the heart.

Second, pursue an eternally minded investment strategy. Even though we don't have a direct command to give a certain percentage or at certain intervals, there is wisdom in developing some kind of regular, systematic way of giving. Giving as you have "decided in your own heart" means not waiting until the pressure to give is there but going with your gut. It means having a plan for your giving.

As it concerns giving to your church, having a regularity to your giving serves the church by blessing it with a somewhat predictable income stream so leaders can make plans accordingly. Deciding in advance what you want to give may turn out to be 10 percent, but it does not need to be the rule. There does seem to be something about the principle of proportionate giving that is biblical. (1 Cor. 16:2; 2 Cor. 8:12; Mark 12:41–44).[11]

Your motivation for giving shouldn't be temporal reward, but eternal reward. This is what I call having an eternally-minded investment strategy. Like all aspects of stewardship, our financial stewardship should acknowledge that the ultimate payoff for how we invest what's been entrusted to us is not in temporal blessings but in the riches of heaven.

Third, enjoy your financial blessings. One idea that's often lost in the discussion of Christian giving is the biblical instruction to enjoy our blessings.

Many Christians feel bad about spending any money on themselves. Maybe you have a vague sense of guilt for wearing any clothing that cost more than a potato sack, for eating out, or for owning anything but the cheapest car. But this attitude toward money has more in common with the

---

11 Tilley. "Stewardship."

Roman Catholic monastic movement than the Bible. The Scriptures commend the enjoyment of God's blessings, and that includes financial blessings.

The apostle Paul gave specific instructions for the rich whom Timothy would have been ministering to in Ephesus. In First Timothy 6:17–19 he told Timothy to relay four specific instructions to the "rich in this present world."

1. Don't be arrogant.

2. Don't set your hope on money.

3. Be rich in good works.

4. Be generous.

You'll note that he did not tell them it was wrong for them to be rich. Previously, Paul had warned about the dangers of wanting to become rich (1 Tim. 6:9; Prov. 23:4–5). But there is a difference between having wealth and idolizing it.

So those who do have wealth must not take pride in it as if their having it was anything more than the blessing of God on their life. Nor are they to set their hopes on what Paul calls "the uncertainty of riches" (1 Tim. 6:17).

As we've already discussed, too often we think that if we just had a little more, then we'd be safe and secure. Instead, Paul says that even the financially rich are to set their hopes "on God, who richly supplies us with all things to enjoy" (6:17).

That little statement, "Who richly supplies us with all things to enjoy" is packed with meaning. Don't miss this. God is the one who will provide us with the temporal necessities we need to survive—things like clothing and food. That's the promise of Matthew 6:25–34.

However, God does not bless us financially for utilitarian purposes alone. God gives us all things richly that we might be generous with them, but also that we might enjoy them.

Too many believers carry an overwhelming sense of guilt for enjoying anything in life. They act as if God is some cosmic killjoy who has laced every blessing with a booby trap to trick us into sin. But that is not the case! God, our great provider, wants us to enjoy what He blesses us with and that includes financial blessing.

There is such a thing as a sinful love of the world (1 John 2:15–17). But there is also a non-sinful, God-glorifying way to enjoy temporal blessings. The Puritan Richard Baxter bluntly wrote, "All love for earthly good is not a sin. Their sweetness is a drop of his love and they have his goodness imprinted on them. They kindle our love for him as love tokens from our dearest friend. Loving them is a duty, not a sin."[12]

There is a world of difference between trusting in or idolizing earthly enjoyments and rejoicing in them as a blessing from God. And again, that difference is our heart. Every blessing you experience is a witness of God's goodness to you. "Yet He did not leave Himself without witness, in that He did good and gave you rains from heaven and fruitful seasons, satisfying your hearts with food and gladness" (Acts 14:17).

These blessings—which include financial blessings—should not be repudiated as sinful indulgences but enjoyed to the glory of God.

When it comes to material blessings God has not called us to a vow of poverty but to a heart of generosity and enjoyment. Some have trouble seeing how both can be true, but they meet most beautifully in the metaphor of stewardship.

The King has left you with riches to care for. You are to use His resources to improve and expand His kingdom and provide for the other stewards of the household with an open hand and a cheerful heart (Luke 19:9; Rom. 12:13). But like the ox, you are also allowed to eat and enjoy the fruit of your own labors (1 Tim. 5:18). We glean even as we gather. And when we approach financial stewardship with the right heart, we lay up for ourselves treasures in heaven that far surpass whatever earthly treasure we may be entrusted with (Matt. 6:19–20).

ONE HABIT: KEEP A BUDGET

How can we practically discharge this duty of financial stewardship? The scope of our financial stewardship is vast. We are obligated to provide for our families, save for the future, give to others, and render to Caesar through taxes. And that is all in addition to daily necessities that require our finances—things like food, clothing, bills, and other essentials.

We must trust God in all these things. But faithful stewards are proactive with their finances. We put trust into action by accompanying our faith with diligent planning. One very practical way to ensure that you are a faithful steward of your financial resources is to keep a budget.

I have been surprised by how many Christians simply do not keep a budget of any kind. They just wing it every month. Somehow it all works out; the ends always find a way to meet.

---

12 Richard Baxter, *Voices from the Past: Puritan Devotional Readings,* ed. Richard Rushing (Carlisle, PA: Banner of Truth, 2015), 294.

But is that how we judge faithful stewardship? The bills got paid this month, so we're good? No, faithful stewards plan ahead.

As we have already seen, when it comes to giving, we are to do so as we have decided in our hearts. That means making a plan in advance for giving. So at the very least that means setting some money aside to give. In other words, you need a budget. And I believe there is wisdom in having a budget, not just for giving, but for your whole financial outlook.

If you are new to this, don't be intimidated. A budget does not need to be complicated. And it does not need to be a spreadsheet dictator for your life. The best place to start is simply to use either a budgeting software or a spreadsheet on your computer to determine how much you want to try to save and give each month—again deciding on a percentage of your income may be helpful here but not necessary.

For example, if you determine in your heart to set aside 10 percent for savings and 10 percent for giving and use the rest for living expenses, that might seem frightening if you haven't done it before. But I've found again and again that creativity thrives under constraint. You'll be surprised how creative you will get with saving money if you must work with just 80 percent of what you had before. So, start there.

And when it comes to how to budget for the normal expenses of your life, I've found it most helpful to start by first tracking your spending for a couple of months before actually trying to live by a budget.

Just group the transaction you make into broad categories like "Food," "Housing," "Gas," etc. This lets you get a picture of where the money is going, and you will likely discover some surprises in this process.

Many people, for example, have no idea just how much money they are spending eating out each month until they track it. Once you see the patterns, then you can create a more proactive budget that assigns a specific amount to each of those categories, and you can set a goal of not spending more than you allot to each.[13]

The most important part of a budget is not the saving, the giving, or the spending—it's the trusting. It's the silent prayer of Matthew 6:11, "Give us this day our daily bread." That's the heart attitude we want to have as we approach our finances.

---

13 My personal favorite tool for budgeting is an app called "You Need a Budget." It works like a digital cash envelope system and lets you easily move money from one category to another to cover overages instead of like a typical Excel budget that might make you want to give up if you spend too much in a certain category.

Thinking about money can easily invite worry about the future, and even giving can bring anxiety. "What if I don't have enough this month?" But trusting that it's the Master's money, not yours, and that He knows exactly what you need and is more than able to provide it is the heart of faith that allows you to be massively generous without being tremendously anxious.

Conclusion

Financial stewardship, like all stewardship, is a matter of recognizing that all that we have belongs to God. It's the Lord's money. And faithfulness in stewarding it means using our money in a way that pleases Him. We can give thanks that He has promised to provide for our needs. And those promises should supply us with confidence as we give generously, work faithfully, and trust fully in our great God who provides us all things richly to be enjoyed.

Study Questions:

1. Why do you think finances are often such an uncomfortable topic for Christians?

2. How does the Old Testament concept of tithing relate to how Christians are to give today?

3. Do you have a plan for giving to God? What does that look like?

4. What are some areas of your finances that need to change for you to be a more faithful steward of the money God has entrusted to you?

5. Do you keep a budget? What's one practical next step you could take to improve how you plan your finances for God's glory?

CONCLUSION

So you too, when you do all the things which are commanded you, say,
"We are unworthy slaves; we have done only *that which we ought to*
have done."

Luke 17:10

THE ROMAN CATHOLIC Church has a term for when Christians go beyond what God requires. They call it performing "works of supererogation." The idea is that God has called all believers to a certain standard of Christian living, but some believers can rise above that bar.[1]

According to the classical teaching of the Church, they taught that those saints who went above and beyond the call of duty, as it were, by these acts of supererogation were contributing to a "treasury of merit." This acted like a sort of heavenly stockpile of extra credit good works.

In the Roman Catholic system, which required the blasphemous addition of works to earn one's salvation, normal Christians could draw upon these good works reserves through the system of indulgences to make up for their own, or a friend's, moral shortcomings. In short, for the low, low price of just a few crowns you could buy your sister-in-law out of purgatory.

When Martin Luther first began poking at the Roman Catholic Church, this system and indulgences and supporting doctrines like supererogation were first pierced by the nail which affixed his Ninety-five Theses to that door in Wittenberg. But why do we bring up the topic of supererogation here in the epilogue to a book on life stewardship? Works of supererogation don't exist. Yet even Protestant Christians, when they begin to take stewardship seriously, can be tempted to act as though they do. Here's what I mean.

Stewardship *is* the Christian life. It's our responsibility, it's our joy, and it's our crown. But as much a privilege as it is to be a steward of God, we

---

1   Hugh Chisholm, "Supererogation," *Encyclopedia Britannica* Vol. 26, 11th ed., (Cambridge: Cambridge University Press, 1911), 111.

must always retain a certain humility regarding our role in God's story. We enjoy the honor of participating in His mission, but we are only supporting characters. He is the hero. And we would do well to not forget our place.

The call to stewardship is not a call to an extraordinary Christian life but an ordinary one. In an age when "comfortable Christianity" has taken root in the Western church, those who rise to the call of biblical stewardship may feel they're in a lonely place, even among Christian friends. But the worst mistake a believer can make is to take hold of the charge of Christian stewardship, begin to live more faithfully, and then start to see himself or herself as better than fellow servants. We act as if the basic obedience from former rebels like us merits a pat on the back, as though our servanthood represented some kind of work of supererogation.

Jesus checked this attitude in His disciples in Luke 17 with the following rhetorical question, ""Which of you, having a slave plowing or tending sheep, will say to him when he has come in from the field, 'Come immediately and sit down to eat'?" (17:7). Our Lord supplied the obvious answer, "Will he not say to him, 'Prepare something for me to eat, and properly clothe yourself and serve me while I eat and drink; and afterward you may eat and drink'?" (17:8).

This is not cruelty or unkindness. This is just the proper order of the master-servant relationship. Servants serve. They don't expect special treatment or praise for doing their job. "He does not thank the slave because he did the things which were commanded, does he?" (17:9). The implied answer is no.

Jesus calls us to have this attitude as His stewards. No matter how obedient we are, we will never be able to say that we have done more than was required. "So you too, when you do all the things which are commanded you, say, 'We are unworthy slaves; we have done only that which we ought to have done'"(17:10).

Faithfulness in life stewardship is a call to responsibility. It is not glamorous or heroic; it is service. So, my fellow steward, let us commit to do our duty with humility and gratitude because our Master is worthy of our best, and our best is the minimum that faithful stewardship requires of us.

But let us also take courage. For we serve at the pleasure of a good Master, a Master who, though we don't deserve it, rewards our faithfulness. When we meet Him on that great and wonderful day and present to Him the only thing we can present to Him, the lives we've lived as living sacrifices, I pray that we would all hear those blessed words, "Well done, good and faithful servant. You have been faithful over a little; I will set you over much. Enter the joy of your master."

PUBLICATIONS

Fort Washington, PA 19034

This book is published by CLC Publications, an outreach of CLC Ministries International. The purpose of CLC is to make evangelical Christian literature available to all nations so that people may come to faith and maturity in the Lord Jesus Christ. We hope this book has been life changing and has enriched your walk with God through the work of the Holy Spirit. If you would like to know more about CLC, we invite you to visit our website:

www.clcusa.org

To learn more about the remarkable story of the founding of
CLC International, we encourage you to read

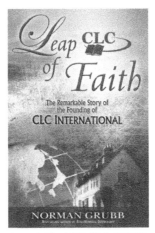

LEAP OF FAITH

Norman Grubb
Paperback
Size 5^1/$_4$ x 8, Pages 248
ISBN: 978-0-87508-650-7
ISBN (*e-book*): 978-1-61958-055-8

THE INSTITUTE FOR THE CHRISTIAN LIFE

A MINISTRY OF
THE MASTER'S SEMINARY

(Scan the QR code below, or go to https://institute.tms.edu)

**Try any one of our online courses for 50% off
(use the promo code WELCOME2ICL).**

We support church leaders through an online certificate program that promotes sound doctrine and a biblical philosophy of ministry. The online courses for the Institute are designed to bring all the vital areas of Bible training, theological instruction, and practical ministry into the pew. We want to make these indispensable tools accessible to laypeople at all levels of church leadership and spiritual maturity. This program will be an aid to new believers as well as seasoned saints.

Each class is broken into one-hour weekly lessons with short quizzes, reading assignments, and group discussion guides. These hours are broken down into shorter segments, taken at any pace, for the convenience of working professionals and busy parents.

Best of all, these lessons are taught by the professors of The Master's Seminary and other distinguished guest lecturers. In that sense, the online courses from the Institute bring the quality of a seminary education into your living room.

Every believer needs to be a theologian. We want to help you fulfill this high and holy calling to the glory of God.